Imaginary Realities

Imaginary Realities

The Psychology of Everyday Delusions

JEFFREY JENSEN ARNETT

OXFORD
UNIVERSITY PRESS

OXFORD
UNIVERSITY PRESS

Oxford University Press is a department of the University of Oxford.
It furthers the University's objective of excellence in research, scholarship,
and education by publishing worldwide. Oxford is a registered trade mark of
Oxford University Press in the UK and in certain other countries.

Published in the United States of America by Oxford University Press
198 Madison Avenue, New York, NY 10016, United States of America.

CIP data is on file at the Library of Congress.

ISBN 9780197817377

DOI: 10.1093/9780197817407.001.0001

Printed by Marquis Book Printing, Canada

The manufacturer's authorized representative in the EU for product safety is
Oxford University Press España S.A. of Parque Empresarial San Fernando de Henares,
Avenida de Castilla, 2 – 28830 Madrid (www.oup.es/en or product.safety@oup.com).
OUP España S.A. also acts as importer into Spain of products made by the manufacturer.

FSC www.fsc.org MIX Paper | Supporting responsible forestry FSC® C103567

Contents

"There is only *one* world, and that world is false, cruel, contradictory, misleading, senseless... We need lies to vanquish this reality, this 'truth,' we need lies *in order to live*... That lying is a necessity of life is itself a part of the terrifying and problematic character of existence."

Friedrich Nietzsche, *The Will to Power*

"There is no absurdity so palpable that one could not fix it firmly in the head of every man on earth provided one began to imprint it before his sixth year by ceaselessly rehearsing it before him with solemn earnestness."

Arthur Schopenhauer, *Essays and Aphorisms*

"We are all tellers of tales. We each seek to provide our scattered and often confusing experiences with a sense of coherence by arranging the episodes of our lives into stories."

Dan McAdams, *The Stories We Live By*

"Through un-truth, through counter-factuality, man violates an absurd, confining reality, and his ability to do so is at every point artistic, creative. We secrete from within ourselves the grammar, the mythologies, of hope, of fantasy, of self-deception without which we would have been arrested at some rung of primate behavior or would long since have destroyed ourselves... We speak, we dream ourselves free of the organic trap."

George Steiner, *Creative Falsehood*

Preface

The seeds for this book began germinating 50 years ago, when I was 18 years old, living at home and working for a year before going to college. During that year I read whatever happened to be lying around the house, and, my parents being quite educated and intellectually curious, those books included some that had a hefty load of ideas, literally and figuratively.

One book that left a deep mark on my thinking was *The Anatomy of Human Destructiveness*, by Erich Fromm, a German psychoanalyst.[1] Fromm was one of many Jewish intellectuals of the time whose worldview was forged by World War II and the Holocaust. There was a lot in that book about the psychology of Hitler and Nazi Germany, as well as other mass atrocities. It made for some heavy reading for an 18-year-old, and I found much of it both shocking and deeply troubling. I had grown up in a comfortably middle-class family in suburban Detroit and had developed a blithely optimistic view of humanity. Fromm's book shocked me out of it, with an impact that remains with me to this day.

The following year, my freshman year at Michigan State University, I started out as a journalism major because I liked to write, but I decided to take an introductory psychology course just for fun. It turned out to be a very unusual course. The main text was Sigmund Freud's *Introductory Lectures on Psychoanalysis*.[2] Freud was already out of favor in psychology, so this must have been about the only introductory psychology course in the world that used that book as its central text. I loved it! The central insight of the book, and really of Freud's entire oeuvre, that our most important motivations are due to unconscious forces we do not understand, rang true to me and seemed to illuminate a great deal of human behavior. According to Freud, happiness and peace of mind will always be elusive for us, because there will always be an uncomfortable tension between our unconscious motivations for sex and aggression and the restraints of living in a society where those motivations must be either tightly regulated or banished altogether. Nearly 50 years later, I have a much more mixed view of Freud and his legacy, but I continue to be persuaded by his essentially tragic view of the human condition.

A third book I read about that time that had an enduring influence on my thinking was Friedrich Nietzsche's *Thus Spoke Zarathustra.*[3] The book is Nietzsche's philosophy in the form of a biblical-style fable of an ascetic sage who wanders about, mostly alone, and ponders human behavior and the human condition. It contains many brilliant aphorisms, such as "Mistrust all in whom the impulse to punish is powerful" and "[M]an has felt too little joy. That alone is our original sin." I loved and was inspired by Nietzsche's lively intellectual spirit, even though he, too, saw the human condition as essentially tragic, as we are prone to misperceptions of ourselves and others that lead to our unhappiness and theirs.

These three pessimists were my biggest early intellectual influences. All of them were big thinkers, and I wanted to be one of them. I switched my major to psychology and took other courses that introduced me to other big thinkers, such as William James. But when I graduated it turned out there were no job listings for aspiring big thinkers. I decided to go to graduate school in developmental psychology, an arena where my optimism sprang back as a motivation to identify early risk factors in children and ameliorate them before they became entrenched.

I forgot all about big ideas for a while. The nature of science, and of academia generally, is to press you toward specialization, and gradually my interests landed on the age period from 18 to 29 that had not been much studied at that time, some 35 years ago now. After interviewing 18- to 29-year-olds for years I proposed a new life stage term of "emerging adulthood" for this period, because I wanted to write about them and neither "adolescence" nor "young adulthood" seemed to fit them well. This has turned out to be a big idea in psychology. Researchers all around the world embraced it with enthusiasm, and today it is a thriving international field. I devoted about 25 years to developing the theory, doing the foundational research, and supporting and mentoring a worldwide community of talented young scholars.

About five years ago, I decided not to write about emerging adulthood any more. By then I had been writing about it for nearly three decades, and I had said about all I wanted to say about it. Also, because I started the field, I felt I loomed over it too much, and I wanted to clear out so that other people could shine—as they have, and do, and will.

So what next for me, then? I am not ready to sit on the porch in a rocking chair all day, and probably never will be. I decided to return to the big questions that had originally inspired me to become a psychologist: What is our essential psychological nature? Why do we have so much trouble finding peace and happiness as individuals, and why is there so much conflict between us in groups? We are capable of rationality, so why do we so often abandon the rational and embrace the irrational? How and why could delusional thinking be such a deep and pervasive part of our psychology, when you might assume it would be inimical to our success and survival in the world? I had been thinking about these questions for a half-century and reading widely looking for possible answers, so I was ready to write about them. This book is the result.

It is not just scholars of the past like Fromm, Freud, and Nietzsche who have influenced my thinking and have shaped the content of this book. There are also many current scholars who address big questions about the psychology of human nature and provide important insights. Three recent books that provide notable contrasts to mine are *Sapiens: A Brief History of Humankind*, by Yuval Noah Harari; *The Uses of Delusion: Why It's Not Always Rational to Be Rational*, by Stuart Vyse; and *The Story Paradox: How Our Love of Storytelling Builds Societies and Tears Them Down*, by Jonathan Gottschall.

Sapiens is a broad and breezy summary of human history, from its evolutionary origins to the present.[4] Like me, and like many generations of philosophers and historians and psychologists before us, Harari emphasizes that for humans reality is socially constructed and often contains fabricated elements. However, as a historian his focus and the base of knowledge he draws from is much different than mine. He devotes whole chapters to the rise of agriculture (he thinks we would be better off as hunter-gatherers) and the creation of the modern finance system, whereas my book includes chapters on psychological topics like anxiety, moral egoism, joy, and humor that he touches on barely or not at all. We both discuss imaginary aspects of human social thinking, but he emphasizes the constructive and rational consequences of this capacity, such as social agreement on the value of money, whereas my emphasis is on the distorted and delusional consequences. We also disagree on many things; for example, I find his tirade against the rise of agriculture to be bizarre and unconvincing. Nevertheless, I invite all the millions of readers of *Sapiens* to read my book, too, and see which of us you think makes the stronger arguments.

In *The Uses of Delusion*, Stuart Vyse charts the many ways delusions can be beneficial to psychological functioning.[5] Delusions confer a sense of control, which may be illusory but nevertheless has real positive effects on our behavior and well-being. They help us endure our disappointments and losses by allowing us to sustain a high opinion of ourselves. In couple relationships, the ones who idealize each other are more likely to endure. Vyse's book is well-informed and full of insights. However, his view of the functions of delusions is more positive than mine. I recognize that imaginary realities have many useful practical functions, as Vyse does, but my emphasis is much more on the threats that delusions present to our individual and collective functioning. Also, Vyse's book draws mainly from research and theory in psychology, whereas mine combines psychological insights with ideas and information from anthropology, philosophy, and history. Our intended audiences are also somewhat different. Vyse's book is mainly a work of academic psychology, whereas I hope my book will attract a broader audience in addition to psychologists.

Gottschall is one of many theorists and researchers who have mined the theme of "narratives" and "stories" over the past 30 years. His background is in literary studies, and he brings a literary sensibility to *The Story Paradox*.[6] For example, in one chapter he discusses "the universal grammar" of our stories, including "characters trying to resolve predicaments" as well as plots with "a deep moral basis." His emphasis is mainly on the collective stories we tell, in myths, legends, and "historical" accounts of our common past within any culture. He integrates insights powerfully from a wide range of fields and considers not only how stories help us "make sense of the world" but how they are vehicles for "fabricating dangerous nonsense." Gottschall's perspective is very valuable, and I recommend his book with enthusiasm, but my emphasis will be more on how imaginary realities pervade all aspects of our daily lives, not just the collective stories we tell. My perspective also has more psychology in it, with chapters on topics like anxiety, morality, and joy that are mostly missing from his book.

Imaginary Realities is a complex blend of my early influences, my recent influences, and other reading and ruminations that have occupied me for the past half-century. It represents my conclusions about psychology and the human condition after 40 years in academic life and 68 years as a human. In a nutshell, my main conclusion is that we are strongly disposed to creating a delusional version of ourselves and our social relations and reality itself, at both the group and the individual level. This tendency constantly stirs up trouble, because our imaginary realities are constantly clashing with the imaginary realities of others and perpetually lead us into misperceptions and mistakes, sometimes inspiring acts that are harsh and cruel. Yet this tendency is an absolutely necessary and immutable feature of our psychology because it also provides us with existential comfort in the face of our daily barrage of anxieties, from both present causes and threats we imagine, and it promotes warm social bonds and cooperation with others in our ingroups. Imaginary realities infuse everything we think and everything we do, all day long, for everyone, although people and groups vary in just how distorted and fabricated their imaginary realities are. Through education in the scientific method and scientific ways of thinking we can reach truths that are not twisted by our tendency for imaginary realities, but generally we prefer to remain within our cozy cocoon of fabrications.

This is, admittedly, a tragic view of the human condition, in the intellectual tradition of my youthful heroes Fromm, Freud, and Nietzsche. I do not offer any cures for imaginary realities in this book, because I do not think any cures are possible, nor do I think we would want them if there were. This sets me apart from virtually all psychologists today. Our whole field is premised on the optimistic promise of making people feel happier and better about themselves and able to function in healthier ways in their relations with others. I make no such promises and offer no such consolations. Nevertheless, I do believe that there is benefit and value to understanding the indelible features of the psychological human condition, including the tendency for imaginary realities I describe in this book. Once you realize and accept that people are permanently delusional, you stop expecting them to behave reasonably and rationally, and you are no longer unpleasantly surprised when they do not. This insight can make you more compassionate and forgiving of others. Truly, they know not what they do. Jesus and Freud, two very different Jews, were both right about that.

So this is my *Zarathustra*, or perhaps my *Key to All Mythologies*.[7] Its conclusions are not optimistic, but it was a joy for me to write on so many topics I have been thinking about and wanting to write about for so many years. I felt like I was constantly in conversation with all the people I admire intellectually, in the past as well as in the present.

I have many people to thank for their roles in making this book possible. Jon Gottschall provided an informal review of my proposal for Oxford University Press before I submitted it, then a formal review when requested by OUP, and both times gave me valuable encouragement and advice for how to make it better. Hayley Singer at OUP suggested that I change my original draft of the book to focus more on the imaginary realities concept, which was a crucial turning point that greatly improved the manuscript. Hayley also edited the most recent edition of my emerging adulthood book for OUP, and she is one of the talented people who make OUP the greatest university press in the world.

I also owe thanks to my informal team of friends and family members who served as readers and reviewers for the early drafts of chapters of this book. This team includes David Skeel, a professor of law at the University of Pennsylvania and my good friend for over 40 years, since we were both students at the University of Virginia. It's not like he has a lot of extra time left over from his job as a law professor and his roles in his family and church, but he managed to find the time to provide thoughtful comments to all the early chapters. John Sauers, the friend with whom I share a love of tennis, cross-country skiing, Indian food, and literature, gave me early feedback from the perspective of the intellectually curious general reader. Gabe Cain, my young friend who is a phenomenal guitar player and one of the most thoughtful people I know, also took the time to offer comments. My brothers Mike and Pete and my sister Claudia similarly served as exemplary reviewers to represent the kind of intelligent general reader I hope to attract with this book, with Pete also bringing in his perspective as a prominent neuropsychologist at Penn State University. I am really lucky to have such brilliant and generous siblings.

I especially want to recognize the editorial contribution of my son Miles, who provided amazingly detailed and insightful comments on every chapter, multiple times. He is a PhD student at the University of Pennsylvania in biomedical engineering and is also deeply involved in the Science Policy and Diplomacy Group at Penn, yet he made the time to provide remarkably astute insights that have greatly improved each chapter. It turns out that literary editor is among his many extraordinary gifts. Miles, I definitely owe you tickets to at least one Celtics game in return!

This book is dedicated to all these informal reviewers, who I am fortunate to love and be loved by. I also dedicate the book to the spirits of Fromm,

Freud, Nietzsche, and to everyone living today who earnestly seeks the truth about the human condition and insists on looking at that truth straight on. The wonderful paradox of the intellectual life is that even when the truths it reveals are tragic and irremediable, the journey of exploration and discovery is exhilarating.

Jeffrey Jensen Arnett
Worcester, Massachusetts
December 2025

1

The Imagination of a Cultural Animal

In an obscure corner of southwest France there is a cave that descends deep into the earth, more than a half-mile. Once you slip into the narrow entrance you descend into a labyrinth, where all light and sound are soon extinguished, except for the light you bring to illuminate your way and the sound of your feet as you scuffle along gingerly. Up and down the labyrinth goes, then down again, sometimes expanding into large halls, other times so narrow and low you have to lie down and squirm forward on your stomach.

At last, creeping through yet another narrow passageway, you suddenly emerge into a gigantic cave. You hold up your light to reveal an amazing sight. One wall and the entire ceiling are covered with engravings, carved with tools of stone. Nearly all the drawings are of animals that lived in the region over 15,000 years ago, when the art was first created: mammoths, rhinoceroses, bison, wild horses, bears, reindeer, wolverines, and musk oxen, as well as smaller animals such as owls, rabbits, and fish; there is even a detailed drawing of a grasshopper. They are drawn with great skill and vividly. Spears and arrows fly all around them, and many of the animals have been pierced; some have blood spurting from their mouths.

Nearly all of these creatures we can recognize as real animals. However, there is one figure about 15 feet above the floor that is different from the rest (Figure 1.1). It is part human and part beast, or rather, part *beasts*—antlers like a reindeer, strangely round owlish eyes, arms ending in bear claws, a horse-like chest, a bushy tail like a wolf, and a man's penis, legs, and beard. The figure is about 2.5 feet high and 15 inches across, larger than any of the animals on the walls, and it is the only one that is painted (in black) as well as engraved. It is a peculiar figure, to be sure, but one instantly recognizable to anthropologists who have studied tribal societies in recent times: the shaman, a religious leader believed to have magical powers and special knowledge of the spirit world, who dresses in elaborate costumes in order to

Imaginary Realities. Jeffrey Jensen Arnett, Oxford University Press. © Jeffrey Jensen Arnett (2026).
DOI: 10.1093/9780197817407.003.0001

Figure 1.1 The Sorcerer of Trois Frères.

Source: Bégouën and Breuil (1920, p. 45).

set himself apart from others and enhance his access to animal spirits. The researchers who first explored the cave named him "the Sorcerer of Trois Frères" because the cave was named after the three French brothers (*trois frères*) who first discovered it.

What a strange and unusual creature! I mean not the shaman but us, the creature who created the chimerical shaman. You can easily imagine another animal going to great lengths and physical strain in order to reach a food source or a potential mate, but to crawl deep into the earth for the purpose of creating something that never existed except in the imagination, that is something only we humans would do. It's the kind of behavior that makes us "the glory, jest, and riddle of the world!"

But wait—does this example of imaginary realities seem long ago and far away, disconnected from us today? OK, try this one. Many animals are subject to deadly viruses, but only humans are clever enough to have developed vaccines to protect against them. This is only one of many ways we have learned to alter the natural world to suit our purposes. What a species! On the other hand, only humans would come up with the deranged idea that vaccines are some kind of devious plot by nefarious forces, with the ominous potential to cause the disease they are supposed to prevent or render us infertile or imperil us in other ways. What a species.

We humans have the ability to reshape the natural world in amazing ways, but we also have a propensity to imagine our way into bizarre and distorted versions of reality. Anti-vax derangement is a familiar recent example, but there have been innumerable other examples through the millennia. Our societies have typically been oriented around and structured by our myths about invisible supernatural forces and beings and our beliefs about how they can be controlled and appeased. Our wars—and there have been many, many wars—have been fought over territory and resources, yes, but they have been motivated even more often by disputes over which group's conception of imaginary beings is more "true." Our creative arts, too, have often been inspired by the motive to honor and gain the favor of the beings we believe control natural forces and our individual well-being and destiny. We are cultural animals, and our whole lives, the entire structure of our societies, are built on a foundation of cultural beliefs constructed with imaginary realities.

Why do we go to such great lengths to create imaginary realities? What are the psychological motivations that drive us? What practical functions do our imaginary realities serve? What threats do imaginary realities raise—to us in our psychological health, to others in our social behavior, and to the planet at this perilous ecological moment? How can we protect ourselves against these threats? In this book I seek to answer these questions.

What Is "Imaginary"? What Is "Delusional"? Who Decides?

At the outset let me clarify what I mean by "imaginary realities" and "everyday delusions." "Imaginary realities" is a paradoxical term for our paradoxical psychology. When we speak of reality we mean the world *as it really is*, irrespective of how we perceive it or interpret it. So how can any reality be imaginary? We perceive the world in terms of imaginary realities because our worldviews nearly always have imaginary elements and filters and distortions—even though we habitually believe we are perceiving the world as it really is. Once our culture stamps a worldview on our consciousness in the course of our early socialization, that is what is real to us, no matter how many imaginary elements it contains. We never believe our personal worldview or the collective worldview of our group is imaginary; we take it to be real, and if it includes invisible beings and forces that other people and groups deny, that is because we see a deeper and truer reality that they cannot see or that they refuse to acknowledge. However, "we" can easily see that what "they" believe to be real is in fact imaginary, false, even ludicrous. This is one of the ways we know that all cultural belief systems are imaginary, that we believe they describe reality only when we are safely inside them psychologically; anyone outside of them can easily see that they are imaginary. No one today has any trouble seeing that the Sorcerer of Trois Frères did not really have antlers, bear claws, a wolf tail, and the power to summon animals to be killed and devoured.

Imaginary realities include a wide range of religious beliefs, most commonly the belief in invisible supernatural beings who influence human affairs and can be called upon for aid and appeased to avoid their wrath, and the belief in a soul that inhabits the body but is not identical with it and can survive when the body dies. But "imaginary realities" is a much broader concept than religious beliefs. It also includes magical beliefs, that is, beliefs that by knowing the right rituals and procedures we can influence the natural world and other people and our own body (without invoking the intervention of supernatural beings). Imaginary realities also include creative but mistaken interpretations of natural phenomena. The anti-vax example is only one of innumerable errors we have made in our recorded history in our strenuous efforts to make sense of a physical reality that is often mystifying, shocking, and painful. This includes inventing explanations for natural disasters such as floods, famines, and plagues in a desperate attempt to end them and prevent them from happening again. Conspiracy theories are a related theme of our imaginary realities. In our continuous search to understand why things happen we often invent relations between people and events that are not true but that provide a psychologically satisfying explanation. Above all we hate to admit that we do not know why things happen, and even more we hate to admit that we cannot control the things that happen to us and those we love. This need to understand and control is a fundamental motivator of our creation of imaginary realities, as we will see. Finally, imaginary realities include our beliefs about the goodness and worthiness of our group in relation to competing groups and the goodness and worthiness of ourselves in relation to others.

A variety of folk beliefs are also part of our imaginary realities. By "folk beliefs" I mean everyday delusions that we employ to make sense of events and help us navigate our way through our daily lives. In every society, people commonly believe in lucky or unlucky numbers, objects, places, and so on. Folk beliefs also include beliefs in fate, destiny, and that "some things are meant to be," never mind by who or what. A popular American folk belief in this vein today is the belief that you can be whatever or whoever you want to be. Although the evidence against this statement is abundant and readily at hand for each of us—I will never be able to dunk a basketball, no matter how intensely I wish I could do so—believing it is motivating and encouraging and can even make it at least partially self-fulfilling in some cases.

The phrase "everyday delusions" in this book's subtitle also merits some explaining. Delusions are false beliefs about how the world works. The term has a long history in psychology to describe how people with serious mental illnesses often have false beliefs, for example, that someone is trying to poison them or that someone important or famous is in love with them. My point in using "everyday delusions" is that we all rely on false beliefs in our everyday lives in order to make the world more satisfying and comprehensible than it actually is. Our false beliefs are not usually at the extreme of those of people who suffer from psychoses, but they are nevertheless creative distortions of raw reality. Unlike for people with psychoses, our everyday delusions do not interfere with our ability to function normally in the world; *they make it possible.* For a variety of reasons I will explain, the capacities of our big brains make the events around us—especially the possible events we imagine and fear—potentially overwhelming. Imaginary realities assuage these fears by making the world seem comprehensible and partially controllable.

In short, distortions of reality are not a bug in our psychology; they are a deeply entrenched and permanent feature. Derangement is our natural condition, with a range from slight to psychotic. This tendency can be modified by education in scientific principles, but it cannot be eradicated. And truly, we would not want it to be.

Who am I to say that none of the beliefs I include under the umbrella of the imaginary realities concept are valid, that they are all imaginary? Beliefs like "luck" are pretty easily refuted, as the laws of probability are well-established. But what about gods and other supernatural forces? Arnett, you can't prove they do *not* exist. That's true. And I am no atheist but an agnostic. Atheists are left with the thorny problem of explaining why there is something instead of nothing. We agnostics admit we don't know, about this and a lot of things. But we do know that a lot of our beliefs about imaginary realities, from gods to magic to folk beliefs, are explainable on the basis of what we know now about human psychology. That is what this book is about.

Is there anything that is *not* imaginary in our interpretations of our experience? Is there any underlying truth that we can grope our way to, or is all truly illusion? Certainly there is much we grasp that is true and factual and verifiable, not just perceived to be so. From our first mastery of fire to our cultivation of plants and animals that could be domesticated to today's dizzying world of international travel and instant worldwide communication, we have proved ourselves a species remarkably adept at practical applications of intelligence, especially in the 500 years since we began to understand and apply scientific methods. But only a small proportion of us needs to understand how to create these marvels in order for all of us to enjoy them, and even highly accomplished people have their imaginary realities outside the narrow realm of their scientific or technological expertise. On the other hand, even people immersed daily in imaginary realities—most of us, most of the time, in most places—are able to conduct a reality-based daily life that includes preparing food, personal grooming, work-related tasks, interpersonal relations, and so on.

People cherish their imaginary realities, on both the group and individual levels. These are the beliefs they hold most dear and guide their lives by. Because my goal here is to illuminate the psychological sources of imaginary realities, to demystify them, I realize I risk offending pretty much everyone in the course of this book. But I hope not; that is not my intent. I don't scoff at imaginary realities in this book. I don't heap contempt on humanity for embracing them. On the contrary, I think we have excellent psychological reasons for embracing them and that nearly all of us would be lost without them. My modest hope is that by casting light on imaginary realities and pondering their psychological sources we can make the worst of them less harmful.

The imaginary realities concept extends broadly over many areas of psychology as well as parts of philosophy, anthropology, sociology, history, even arts and humanities. In this book I am not going to summarize all the ideas and research across all the different fields and domains I draw from, as that would distract too much from the new ideas I am proposing. Instead, my focus will be on imaginary realities as a new umbrella concept that seeks to draw attention to our broad psychological tendency to create a fabulous version of the world that is more understandable and controllable than the world in its raw state. I will also apply the imaginary realities concept to a variety of areas not previously highlighted for their distortions of reality: our anxieties, morality, joy, and humor. In the final chapter I will apply the concept to some vexing issues of our present and future: ecological damage, artificial intelligence, and the extension of the human lifespan.

A Uniquely Cultural Animal

Of key importance to understanding imaginary realities is recognizing that we are the only cultural animal.[1] Other animals, including our closest primate relatives, have many innate patterns of behavior and are born with a range of propensities to learn the behaviors and skills that will enable them to survive. These patterns and behaviors were selected for across many generations, as the young of the species whose innate qualities were best suited to the ecological niche into which they were born were the ones who were most likely to survive long enough to reproduce and leave young of their own in the next generation.

All other animals have evolved to be adapted to a specific ecological niche over many generations. Their instincts and propensities are suited to that niche. But humans are extraordinarily and uniquely different. Although we have some instincts and propensities of our own that evolved in the ecological niche of the African savannah, they are weaker and more flexible than in any other animal. For a long time after we are born we are able to do very little compared to other animals. We not only have the fewest instincts and the weakest propensities, but we have the longest period of immaturity of any animal. Instead of an array of instincts and strong propensities suited to a specific ecological niche, we have the greatest capacity for learning, by far, due to our extraordinarily large and complex brains. Consequently, we have been able to learn to live in virtually any ecological niche, all over the world, from mountains to deserts, from tropical rain forests to the frozen arctic. In each place, in every place, we create cultures to guide our learning and behavior. Invariably, our cultures are founded in an imaginary reality that explains who we are individually and collectively and that adds social and psychological power to cultural prescriptions for behavior.

Imaginary Realities and the Creation of Cultures

We are uniquely cultural. Some biologists and evolutionary psychologists disagree.[2] They have proposed that other great apes, whales, dolphins, elephants, and even some species of birds have "cultures," because these animals have distinctive learned patterns of behavior and even some simple tools and technologies. For example, biologists observed that Japanese monkeys on the island of Koshima had developed a learned behavioral pattern of washing their sweet potatoes before eating them. Sweet potatoes are their main food, but they had always been vexed by the dirt they would inevitably taste in the course of eating them. Then one monkey, whom the biologists called Imo, discovered that washing a potato in salt water not only removed the dirt but made it tastier. Soon all the monkeys had embraced this new "technology," and it was maintained in subsequent generations.

"Monkeys have cultures!" declared the biologists. Sorry, no. This is a fascinating and entertaining example, but one simple learned behavior does not make a culture. It is deeply mistaken to reduce "culture" to patterns of learned behavior, because this strips away the essence of it. What makes culture so important and so uniquely human is that it is first and foremost about shared beliefs in an imaginary reality—a world we create from our imagination but that we believe to be real. It would be culture if Imo and his followers believed that potatoes had been bestowed on them by the gods, that washing potatoes is holy and should be done ceremoniously, and that other groups of monkeys who eat their potatoes without washing them are stupid and barbaric and deserve contempt. My definition of culture as based first and foremost on shared beliefs is drawn from a long tradition in anthropology and a more recent consensus in cultural psychology.[3] No beliefs, no culture. Only humans have beliefs, so only humans have cultures.

Our status as the only cultural animal is at the heart of my conception of imaginary realities. It is our compulsion to create cultures that is the foundation of our imaginary realities, and it is our innate readiness to learn the ways of the culture we find ourselves born into that prepares us to embrace wholeheartedly whatever imaginary reality we are taught from infancy onward. Through the cultural creation of imaginary realities, we develop beliefs that include prescriptions for how to fulfill our place in the social order of our society. Furthermore, the imaginary reality we learn enables us to reorganize and reshape a harsh, confusing, potentially overwhelming world into something we believe we can understand and control, or at least endure.

Our predisposition for cultural learning goes so deep into the psychology of human nature that in the course of childhood we come to think of our culture's imaginary world as real, natural, and inevitable, rather than simply one invented alternative among many. By the time we reach adulthood we have a stable set of cultural beliefs, and within cultural groups these shared beliefs promote social cohesion and social order, allowing us to coordinate our daily activities with others. Across groups we are culturally creative, and the range of different imaginary realities we have invented is remarkable. However, within groups we tend to thwart and punish attempts at cultural innovation. We resist changing our beliefs when circumstances change; we resist recognizing them as imaginary realities rather than as a true understanding of the nature of the physical and supernatural worlds. This resistance arises partly from regarding our cultural ways as part of a powerful supernatural order that cannot be questioned.

A related aspect of our cultural nature as a species is that it frequently leads us to regard ourselves as more than one species. That is, the psychological tendency to regard our culture's imaginary reality as emphatically true and of ultimate value frequently leads to a conclusion that is only us, in our culture, who are truly human. Those people adjacent to us, with their strange, peculiar, unnatural customs and beliefs, are . . . something else, something clearly inferior. Our cultural identity is thus formed in part by distinguishing our group's imaginary realities from the beliefs of other groups. The distinctions we make between us and them are not merely cognitive but *moral*. Our beliefs are not just different from those of other groups but better, superior, the right beliefs, the one true reality. It is easy for us to see that the beliefs of people in other groups are false—we often regard them as laughably false and enjoy ridiculing them—whereas our beliefs are true, the ultimate truth, and if you ridicule them you may arouse an angry and perhaps violent response. The psychological tendency to moralize group differences in imaginary realities has enormous consequences for social relations, as we shall see.

Imaginary Realities as Psychological Niches

It may be useful to think of our creation of cultures as the development of *psychological niches.* The concept of "niche construction" is a key part of standard evolutionary theory.[4] Organisms are born into an ecological niche, and they survive or not based on how well their inherited characteristics are adapted to that niche. However, many animals alter their niches. Birds build nests, beavers construct dams, spiders weave webs, lots of animals dig holes for dens. In the course of human evolution, we increasingly made our own niches based on our accumulated cultural knowledge. We learned how to control fire, how to make our own dwellings, how to make clothes that would protect us from extremes of cold, how to domesticate plants and animals for our purposes, and how to process foods in ways that would broaden the range of things we could eat. Eventually we created societies and civilizations that entirely altered the ecological conditions that influence our survival and reproduction.

But in the course of our evolution we developed the capacity to create not only physical niches but psychological niches—our imaginary realities. During the evolutionary development of *Homo sapiens*, just as our physical reality was often too harsh and we needed to ameliorate it with inventions such as dwellings and clothes, our psychological reality was also too harsh, full of threats both real and imagined. Creating imaginary realities has often meant making our psychological surroundings even more fraught with anxiety, because we imagine many threats that do not exist, but it also helps ameliorate our fears, because it gives us ways of believing that we can protect ourselves against threats and assures us that we can predict and control them to some extent. Ultimately our imaginary realities promote our survival, because they alter our psychological environment in ways that enable us to cooperate with each other more effectively.

In the course of human evolution, eventually our cultural innovations in creating both physical and psychological niches accumulated to the point where we rely on them not just to thrive but to survive. We quite literally cannot live without our cultural beliefs and practices, from cooking to counting to cultural beliefs that explain who we are and our place in the natural and supernatural worlds, making us unlike any other animal.[5] We are permanently dependent on the cognitive and conceptual worlds we have created, and on our mutual cooperation and coordination in sustaining those worlds and developing them further. Our genes changed as our cultural conditions changed, and for tens of thousands of years we have depended on our cultural inventions and traditions, including our imaginary realities, in order to maintain human life.

Imaginary Realities and Fear of the Future

Research on neuropsychology and brain development holds important insights for understanding why imaginary realities are necessary for a uniquely cultural animal. According to neuropsychologists, the part of the brain that is most distinctively human is the prefrontal cortex, just behind your forehead.[6] The prefrontal cortex is the part of the brain that evolved most recently. It executes many of our most important and distinctively human functions, most notably the capacity to anticipate the future. This ability is of crucial importance to human survival. If you anticipate the coming of winter, you can store food to help survive the months when edible plants are harder to come by and animals are scarce, or you can migrate to warmer climes before winter arrives. If you anticipate where an animal herd habitually gathers, you can hide yourself nearby and then spring upon them when they appear. If you anticipate an attack from another human group, you can protect yourselves or attack them first.

Although anticipating the future is of great value in diverse ways that enhance survival, it also carries a burdensome liability: we experience a great deal of anxiety and stress imagining all the bad things that could happen but never do, and preparing ourselves against threats that never actually materialize. Our imaginary realities are often the source of the threats we anticipate. We fear incurring the displeasure or wrath of imaginary beings, and—across cultures—we go to great lengths to honor them and appease them so that they will be assured of our submission and devotion and thus refrain from inflicting suffering upon us. We imagine the destructive potential of imaginary forces and take elaborate steps to devise methods of protecting ourselves. One example of this that is popular across many cultures is creating amulets that will protect us from the Evil Eye.[7] This is the belief that other people can inflict misfortune, illness, and even death upon us or those we love just by wishing us ill. Creating these amulets is one of the many ways we expend a great deal of our time and resources attempting to protect ourselves from threats that are strictly a product of our imagination.

The amulets example also shows how imaginary realities are not only the source of the threats we fear; they also provide methods for assuaging our anxieties and relieving our stress.[8] There are supernatural and magical forces that will cause us harm if we fail to recognize them, but if we anticipate them and take steps to protect ourselves, we can avoid their harm. The same spirits and gods and forces that threaten to harm us can also be invoked to protect us. So we hope and believe.

Our exceptional ability to anticipate future events is invaluable, but it also threatens to submerge us. There are times when people have such high anxiety that they lose the ability to function. We create imaginary realities not only to quell these anxieties but to provide us with the assurance that the forces that threaten us can be understood and at least partially controlled. As bad as it is to imagine the world as full of threats, worse yet would be to conclude that they are beyond our understanding and there is nothing we can do about them. Throughout our species' history, we have created imaginary realities so that we will not be vanquished by the vast complexity of the world and its infinite potential for doing us harm. We rely on our imaginary realities to console us and to provide a version of the world that is within our capacity to understand.

Imaginary Realities and Explaining Our Suffering

Our amazing brains allow us to imagine potential threats to our survival and well-being and take steps to avoid them. Nevertheless, we have experienced abundant suffering in our species' history, and we do today as well, from diverse sources: disease, famine, attacks from human enemies and animal predators, and natural disasters. The causes of these catastrophic events have often been mystifying and obscure to us. Imaginary realities have been created in part to explain the sources of our suffering and offer us a means to avoid or at least partly control them.

Our capacity for niche construction is impressive, but our capacity for creating psychological niches is equally marvelous and may be equally important for our survival. This is true even though there are aspects of our imaginary realities that seem irrational, bizarre, and sometimes ridiculous. Think again about the Sorcerer of Trois Frères. What possible survival purpose could the creation of the Sorcerer have served? Apparently the people who created it believed its creation was connected to their hunting success, but wouldn't it have made more sense to focus on developing better hunting tools and strategies instead of spending all that time crawling deep into the earth to create the Sorcerer?

But we don't always take the cultural path that makes the most sense. On the contrary, we frequently build whole societies around an elaborate system of cultural beliefs that not only do not seem to promote our physical survival and reproductive success but seem to actively interfere with it.[9] At various times and places in our species' history we have killed female newborns because they were not male; executed captives in order to keep the sun shining; and decided that fish were taboo as a food source (Figure 1.2). Clearly there is more to us than merely an obvious focus on physical survival.

It is crucial to understand our species' evolutionary history and how our cultures and genes coevolved to make us a unique species, but creating cultures triggered a process of innovation that eventually took on a life of its own. Our cultural inventions have certainly helped us survive and thrive in many ways, most obviously in the tools and technologies we have created but also in the cultural beliefs that promote social cohesion and cooperation.

AZTECS SACRIFICING TO THE SUN.

Figure 1.2 The Aztecs believed it was necessary to sacrifice human captives in order to keep the sun shining.

But eventually we became so successful as cultural animals that our brains became big enough and complex enough to develop desires and needs beyond mere survival. Eventually we came to need *meaning* as well. We came to need to be able to explain and understand the world around us, not just survive in it and make use of it. Frequently this need for creating meaning has entailed developing imaginary realities that are irrational and inaccurate but emotionally and socially comforting. Sometimes the need for meaning has even prevailed over the animal need to survive and reproduce.

Imaginary Realities: A Brief History

If our beliefs in imaginary realities have been at the heart of human motivations and how we structure our societies throughout our species' history, of course other thinkers must have observed this over the centuries, and they have, in myriad ways. Over two millennia ago, Plato presented the famous allegory of the cave, whose residents mistake shadows on the wall for the real world. Around the same time, the ancient Epicurean and Stoic philosophers pointed out the many ways we distort and misperceive reality. Much of the ensuing 2,300 years in philosophy have been devoted to pondering our distortions of reality and how to overcome them. Various religious thinkers have emphasized our misconceptions of ourselves and the world, from the Buddhists observing that we are prisoners of our illusions to the Apostle Paul declaring that in this world the best we can do is to see reality "as through a glass, darkly." Over the past century and a half, our propensity for constructing and believing in imaginary realities has been recognized in anthropology and psychology as well.

Imaginary Realities Are Human Universals

Anthropology is an especially rich source of beliefs in imaginary realities. Over the past century and a half, anthropologists have documented the elaborate belief systems created in cultures around the world, invariably including the mysteries of magical forces and supernatural beings. Together, the reports of anthropologists provide invaluable information on imaginary realities. By scanning the world's cultural beliefs, we can gain insights into their common features.

The first list of human universals based on anthropology was compiled by George Murdock in 1945. The list was updated and expanded by Donald Brown in 1991 and 2004.[10] An alphabetical selection is shown in Table 1.1. I have highlighted in bold the ones that have implications of imaginary realities.

Table 1.1 Human universals in anthropology

Age status and term (e.g., child, adult, elder)	Deception	Meal times
Attachments to others	Dominance and submission	**Morality—right and wrong, good and bad**
Baby talk	**Dreams and dream interpretation**	Music—melody and rhythm
Belief in supernatural	Envy	**Myths/narratives/stories**
Beliefs about death	**Ethnocentrism**	Play and toys
Beliefs about disease	Facial expressions (e.g., anger, disgust, fear, happiness, sadness, surprise)	Poetry
Beliefs about fortune and misfortune	Food sharing	Reciprocity (of labor, goods, or services)
Childbirth customs	**Future, attempts to predict**	**Rituals**
Childhood fear of strangers	Gender—males and females seen as having different natures	**Self-image and self-presentation**
Collective identities	Gossip	Sexual regulation
Consciousness—altering it via techniques or drugs	Hope	Shame
Conflict and methods of resolution	Hospitality	Socialization by older kin
Cooking/control of fire	**Ingroup/outgroup distinctions**	**Status hierarchies**
Cooperation	Jokes	**Taboos**
Culture/nature distinction	Leaders	Trade
Dance	**Magic**	Violence—individual and collective
Death rituals	Marriage	**Weather control (attempted)**

It is striking how many of the human universals are based on imaginary realities. All the cultures studied by anthropologists have created beliefs in the supernatural, beliefs about the causes of disease, and beliefs about how to enhance good fortune and avoid misfortune. All cultures have collective identities, based on imaginary realities, and express ethnocentrism based on those identities and beliefs, such as "Our gods are better than your gods." All cultures have myths, narratives, and stories, typically involving the activities of mythical ancestors and supernatural beings and their interventions into human affairs. All attempt to predict the future and control the weather, usually by appealing to supernatural forces and beings. All believe in a moral order, established by divine forces. All have rituals surrounding death, reflecting beliefs in an afterlife. Even many of the universals I have not highlighted in bold have aspects of imaginary realities—for example, dominance and submission are often based on beliefs in a natural order decreed by supernatural beings; music and dance are often created to celebrate or honor imaginary realities; and leaders are often believed to have special access to supernatural powers. The presence of imaginary realities in so many aspects of human universals shows how deeply our beliefs in imaginary realities go into the fundamental psychology of human nature.

Imaginary Realities in the History of Psychology

Psychology has a long history of recognizing the human propensity for imaginary realities, but often indirectly and incompletely. Sigmund Freud was the first in psychology to point to the fundamental unreality and irrationality of our thinking and motivations. According to Freud, we are driven daily by unconscious motives, especially for sex and aggression, and we almost never realize it. Instead, we repress these drives and create a fabric of respectability that conceals what we really need and want, even from ourselves. We also repress and conceal memories of traumatic events, and this repression can result in psychological disorders. Today psychologists regard Freud's claim of the centrality of motives of sex and aggression as simplistic and overstated. Nevertheless, his emphasis on our tendencies for irrationality and for creating a false image of ourselves and the world has continued to resonate in psychology, especially in social psychology.

Much theory and research in social psychology have been devoted to highlighting and conceptualizing the many ways that we distort reality in our social relations. For example, Leon Festinger's theory of *cognitive dissonance* became widely known because most of us have had the experience it encapsulates: holding two incompatible views makes us uneasy, and we seek to resolve this conflict by changing one of them, even if that means distorting reality.[11] In a famous example that inspired the theory, Festinger managed to infiltrate a cult that believed the end of the world was coming on a specific date, and when it did not come they concluded not that they were wrong but that their faith and goodness had saved the world from ruin. This was a good demonstration of how agile our imaginary realities can be when they collide unpleasantly with hard facts. Another concept, *social comparisons*, explains people's tendency to compare themselves favorably to others.[12] Research has shown that people tend to evaluate themselves positively in comparison to "other people," sometimes called the "better than average effect," rating themselves more intelligent, more competent, more friendly, and so on. These and many other social psychology concepts will be applied in the chapters to come by highlighting the ways they represent our tendencies for creating imaginary realities of ourselves and the social world.

Theory and research on the psychology of religion are also germane to imaginary realities, and this field goes back over a century, to William James's book in 1900, *The Varieties of Religious Experience*. James collected all the research that had been done up to that time on the psychology of religion and added his own insights from decades of influential and diverse work in psychology. He emphasized the distortions of reality represented in religious beliefs and the ways that extreme religious beliefs veer sharply into psychopathology and mental illness, but he also claimed that religion motivates many of the behaviors we regard as "highest" and most moral, such as generosity and self-sacrifice. In recent decades, research on the psychology of religion has shown that believing in and practicing a religion is mostly related to good things, such as volunteering, marital satisfaction, personal well-being, and optimism.[13] Today's research has neglected James's spotlighting of the creative distortions of reality typically present in religious beliefs, but my concept of imaginary realities brings back this spotlight and expands it to include not only religious beliefs but many other aspects of how we imagine ourselves and the world.

In recent decades, psychology has devoted a lot of theory and research to the idea that we are prone to creating *narratives*, at both the individual and the collective level, that tie together our experiences into a story that makes sense and can be used as a guide to our social relations and our daily lives. The collective narratives are called *master narratives* and the individual narratives are *personal narratives.* Master narratives are "culturally shared stories that guide thoughts, beliefs, values, and behaviors," according to Kate McLean and Moin Syed, two of the leading theorists in this area.[14] Personal narratives are the individual stories that each person constructs, based on their personal experiences and understandings but also drawn from the materials provided by their culture's master narrative. For example, a girl growing up in rural India may learn the Hindu beliefs of her family and village, contributing to the personal narrative she constructs for herself about how she aspires to live a good life and how she perceives the range of adult pathways open to her (and those not open to her). Master narratives provide a cultural road map for how each life stage should be experienced, providing individuals with material for interpreting what they have experienced so far and for planning what they might experience in the future. Personal narratives help people form an individual identity, derived from cultural master narratives plus their own immediate experiences, that allows them to make sense of their life and understand how they fit into their place and time.

The concept of master and personal narratives and how they are related has a clear connection to the concept of imaginary realities on the cultural and individual levels. However, there is also a stark difference, in that master and personal narratives are very practical concepts, rooted in cultural realities. Master narratives provide a useful guide for developing an individual identity represented in a personal narrative. Narrative psychologists recognize that we are natural creators of stories and tend to emphasize the potential of these stories for redemption and reconciliation.[15]

The idea of imaginary realities also recognizes that the narratives we construct help us coordinate social activities and provide us with sources of meaning and understanding in our own lives. However, imaginary realities have more magical and supernatural elements than is typical in discussions of narratives. Also, the concept of imaginary realities places more emphasis on how our false beliefs can have damaging consequences. Often the stories we construct are fabrications that seriously distort reality in ways that may cause conflict between individuals and groups. Because we are prone to inventing imaginary realities, we are constantly at risk of being led by them into actions that are destructive and disastrous, as we will see in the chapters to come.

Do Imaginary Realities Matter?

It may be fun to entertain ideas about imaginary realities, and it may even be informative, but is it consequential? In the end, isn't this just a frivolous form of intellectual entertainment? Does it really matter what we think about imaginary realities?

Arguably, it would be hard to think of anything that matters more. Our imaginary realities deeply influence how we structure societies, how we approach our relations with other people, and how we form our own identity. For many centuries of Western history the dominant imaginary reality has included the belief that all humans are born sinful and prone to depravity, and consequently the only purpose of our brief and miserable life on earth is to ask forgiveness from supernatural beings and prepare ourselves for our soul's eternal destiny. Every institution and every stage of life, from infancy through old age, was constructed out of this ideological material. More recently, the 19th and 20th centuries of world history were vast contests of imaginary realities, pitting democracy's view that the "natural" tendency of humans is to abuse power and so institutions must be constructed to prevent that tendency, against fascism's view that people respond mainly to dominance and submission and so society is best constructed around a strong leader who must be obeyed, against communism's view that our psychology is a blank slate that can be rewritten without limits to form new humans and a new society however we wish. In every time and place, every human culture, no matter how small or large, is built on imaginary realities.

On a more personal level, too, our imaginary realities perpetually shape our views of ourselves and our relations with others. It matters greatly whether you think of yourself as inherently a kind and generous person who is worthy of love or as an incorrigibly selfish person who deserves to be punished. It matters, too, whether you see other people as basically trustworthy and likeable or as lying adversaries who need to be outwitted. For parents and educators, it matters greatly if you think of children as little angels whose inner goodness needs to be nurtured or as little devils who need to have the devil beaten out of them. For individuals, the dominant imaginary reality of their culture both guides and restricts, supporting and rewarding some paths through life but restricting or blocking off others.

So, I hope you will have fun reading this book, and I hope you will find it intellectually entertaining and provocative. But I hope you will find more in it than that. Above all, reading this book should enable you to recognize the imaginary realities that underlie the cultural beliefs, institutions, rituals, social relations, and individual identities of the people in the culture around you, wherever you live, and in other cultures you visit or read about. The concept of imaginary realities may also enhance your understanding of human history and of current national and international events and conflicts. You may find insights and information here that will lead you to reflect on and perhaps reconstruct your own imaginary reality.

Just don't expect this book to present a cure. There is no cure for our tendency to form and live by imaginary realities, and we would not want it if there were. I realize that psychologists are often expected to propose cures for what ails us. In the course of a career in psychology I have seen many such cures proposed. But this is not that kind of book. Our attraction to imaginary realities cannot be fixed, but at least you will have the consolation of knowing why that is so. This is a book not for potential fixers but for people who yearn to understand better why we are the way we are.

2

The Elements, Origins, Costs, and Benefits of Imaginary Realities

The cultures of the mountainous highlands of Papua New Guinea are diverse, but the people in all of them believe the world is teeming with supernatural agents. The forces of nature are alive, conscious, and intentional, and the spirits of ancestors are ever-present. Each person is believed to have not only a soul but a "spirit familiar," usually an animal or plant spirit, that constantly accompanies them and is there to help and protect them. If this protection fails, shamans can be called upon, as they are believed to have special powers to placate malevolent spirits and to heal people from illnesses that occur due to the use of magic. To the highlanders no illness or death is unexplainable; magic or evil spirits are always involved. The spirits of recently deceased ancestors are especially feared, as they are believed to be angry and vengeful.

Witchcraft has been believed in cultures all over the world for millennia, as a way of understanding why bad things happen when no other explanation is available. From the 13th through the 17th centuries, Europe took these beliefs to an unusual extreme of organization and persecution. Europeans came to believe that witches allied themselves with Satan and his forces to cause a wide range of suffering, from crop failure and loss of livestock to extreme weather events, from sexual dysfunction to illness and death. Because such suffering was always occurring somewhere, the necessity of identifying, prosecuting, and executing witches was urgent and unceasing. In the late 15th century a pair of Catholic monks wrote a treatise called *The Witches' Hammer* detailing the witches' many nefarious methods, then roamed Europe with the support of the Catholic Church, finding and burning witches wherever they went. When the Protestant Reformation arose shortly thereafter, its leaders took up witch prosecution with even more zeal. By the end of the 17th century, when the frenzy finally exhausted itself, hundreds of thousands of witches had been burned, nearly all of them women, many of them mentally ill, elderly, or otherwise vulnerable (Figure 2.1).

Imaginary Realities. Jeffrey Jensen Arnett, Oxford University Press. © Jeffrey Jensen Arnett (2026).
DOI: 10.1093/9780197817407.003.0002

Figure 2.1 During the witch-burning frenzy in Europe, hundreds of thousands of witches were burned.

In today's southeast Asia, including Thailand, Myanmar, and Cambodia, "spirit houses" are popular. The houses range from a few simple wooden boards hammered together and placed on stilts to expensive, ornate houses built by skilled craftspeople. Small figurines, representing various spirits, are placed inside. Spirit beliefs are drawn from ancestor worship, Buddhism, and Hinduism, and the figurines depict revered ancestors, animals, and Hindu demigods. Offerings of food are placed daily before the spirit houses, along with burning incense sticks and garlands of marigolds and jasmine. The spirits are believed to have the power to bring good or bad fortune, depending on their whim as well as on how devoutly they are worshiped. Young people tend to be more interested in social media than in the spirits, but so far spirit houses and the rituals to maintain them persist.

These are three examples, but you could go to any culture in the world, at any time over the past 100,000 years, and find similar imaginary realities, the fantastic tapestry woven between the world-as-it-is and how we understand and experience it. They are all imaginary, and yet we take them to be the truest reality, representing what is most important in life.

Of all the characteristics that make human psychology unique, the most important and consequential is our propensity to create imaginary realities. All creatures have some kind of sensory system—sight, hearing, smell, taste, touch—that allows them to perceive the physical world and respond to it.

But humans are the only creatures who create an imaginary reality that reinterprets the physical world—and the psychological and social worlds—to make them seem comprehensible and at least somewhat controllable.

The world in its raw state is too much for us. There is too much suffering, too much pain and death, and on top of that is the suffering we anticipate and fear for ourselves and our loved ones. Our powerful, complex brains, so adept at envisioning and anticipating future threats, would be overwhelmed by stress and anxiety without some method of organizing and incorporating those threats into a system that reduces their power and makes them manageable. The imaginary realities we create, including our myths, religions, superstitions, magical beliefs, folk theories of nature and medicine, and other supernatural beliefs, provide that method. The invisible forces depicted in imaginary realities may or may not be benevolent, but even if they are not they can be understood and perhaps influenced. Our imaginary realities also provide a framework for organizing social life and enhancing the stability and predictability of social relations. On the individual level, our imaginary realities create a guiding life story that is the basis of a coherent identity that provides meaning and direction.

Imaginary realities serve many important practical functions in structuring social life as well as in making individual psychological functioning smoother and connecting it to the social world. However, what is most striking about imaginary realities is precisely that they are imaginary. They are not accurate representations of how the world functions; they are fabrications and distortions. Yet they are nevertheless at the heart of human psychological and social life. Our challenge in this book will be to understand how this feature of human psychology that is so crucial to it, that goes to the very heart of it, could be so disconnected from the world as it actually is and yet so meaningful, so vital to our psychological functioning. We live by, and are frequently willing to die for, a version of the world that is substantially fabricated.

Calling imaginary realities "imaginary" is meant to be descriptive, not pejorative or insulting. I am not calling them lies or nonsense. I am not trying to talk anyone out of their beliefs in their imaginary reality. The truth is, we need our imaginary realities in order to live. There is nothing shameful or disgraceful about them, although we tend to be contemptuous of the imaginary realities of others; it is easy for us to see, from the outside, that they are merely imaginary. We *all* have imaginary realities, me included—everyone included. If you think you do not, well, I agree with the observation of generations of philosophers that the biggest illusion of all is to believe that you have no illusions.

Now let's examine diverse aspects of imaginary realities, beginning with some examples of the forms they take.

The Elements of Imaginary Realities

As part of our ability to create cultures, we developed the capacity to weave an elaborate imaginary reality between us and the world-as-it-is. Our capacity for constructing imaginary realities is robust, creative, and diverse. Nevertheless, there are certain elements of imaginary realities that appear in cultures all over the world. These elements are combined and shaped in myriad ways to generate the distinctive imaginary realities of specific cultures. Here are some of the elements of imaginary realities that have appeared in many human cultures:

1. *Souls.* In each of us there is a soul that inhabits our body but is not permanently attached to it. The soul represents our individual psychological identity. It is not physical. It existed before the body and will continue to exist after the body dies. During sleep the soul may leave the body to wander among other places and people, and during illness the soul may have temporarily slipped away from the body. When the person dies the soul leaves the body for good. It may enter an afterlife realm, or it may return to life in another body. One common belief is that the souls of our family members in previous generations who have died are still present among us. The souls of these ancestors monitor us, sometimes protect us, and sometimes punish us.
2. *Supernatural beings.* In addition to deceased ancestors, there are many supernatural beings who take a great interest in human affairs and in us personally, monitoring our activities and in some cases rewarding or punishing us for our moral conduct and even for our thoughts. A substantial amount of human activity in all cultures is devoted to appealing to these spirits or gods and attempting to gain access to their power.
3. *Animism and anthropomorphism.* These are similar terms that attribute human psychological and social characteristics to animals, objects, and natural forces. Animism is the belief that nonliving things

(such as the moon or mountains) are alive, and anthropomorphism is the belief that nonhuman things (including animals, objects, and supernatural beings) have human-like thoughts, emotions, and intentions, just like you and me. Both animism and anthropomorphism include the belief that natural and supernatural forces take an interest in human affairs and have the power to help or harm us. It is possible to influence them and appeal to them as you would to another person.

4. *Teleology.* Everything around us has an inherent purpose and intention, as if it were designed for its relation to us. The sun was created to light our way and keep us warm. Animals we find tasty were made for us to eat. Teleology includes beliefs in "fate" and "destiny." Everything happens for a reason. Nothing in human life is random, senseless, or unpredictable. Everything we experience is part of a plan.
5. *Magical beliefs.* Magic is believed in nearly every human culture. It does not require the intervention of a supernatural being but is directed by people who understand how to access supernatural forces. Magical beliefs assume the natural world can be influenced by rituals and practices. For example, agricultural success is believed to be influenced by rituals that control phenomena such as the weather and insect pests. Witchcraft is believed worldwide and typically involves the use of magic to cause good or bad events to happen to others. In many cultures, physical dangers are thwarted with magical rituals, for example, when childbirth or warfare is anticipated. Magical beliefs also include belief in luck, such as lucky numbers, words, or objects that can be used to cause favorable events to come your way.
6. *Spiritual leaders.* There are certain people who have special access to supernatural forces and beings. They have a distinctive title, such as shaman or priest, and are often marked by unusual qualities, such as being born with an extra finger or falling easily into a trance or fit. Trances are a common way of gaining access to supernatural powers and can be induced by fasting, pain, music, dancing, drugs, or meditation. People go to spiritual leaders when they need interventions with supernatural forces, for example, when they are ill.
7. *Thought power.* Thoughts have the power to heal or harm others. Wishing someone good health or good luck can bring favorable events their way. Wishing someone misfortune, illness, or death can harm them.

8. *Immanent justice.* There is a sturdy moral order to the world. Good behavior is rewarded and bad behavior is punished, automatically, although it may take a while for the scales to be balanced. Everyone ultimately gets what they deserve, for better or worse, based on their moral conduct.
9. *Self and identity beliefs.* In addition to the imaginary realities that are collective, each person creates an individual imaginary reality. Each of us has an identity that consists of our beliefs about who we are, the unique features of our personality, our talents and abilities, our deficiencies and limitations, and how others evaluate us. These beliefs are often inaccurate and inflated. In general, we tend to view ourselves as better than others in a variety of ways, especially morally. We tend to remember and exaggerate what we have done that others and ourselves would regard as "good" and minimize or forget the things we have done that others and ourselves would regard as "bad."

These features of imaginary realities have been combined in a wide range of cultural forms. Today over three-fourths of the world's people adhere to one of the four major religions—Christianity, Islam, Hinduism, and Buddhism—and these religions incorporate many of the features of imaginary realities listed above, including souls, supernatural beings, animism and anthropomorphism, teleology, spiritual leaders, and immanent justice (Figure 2.2). In addition, there are many minor religions and innumerable superstitions and folk beliefs that may not be part of an explicit religious system.[1] Imaginary realities are also constructed as part of our many group identities: political, ethnic, linguistic, national, and so on.

In declaring that all humans are prone to constructing imaginary realities, could it be that I am arrogantly assuming for myself the authority to determine what is imaginary and what is real? That's a fair question. I will respond by reiterating that we can all easily see that beliefs that we do not hold ourselves are imaginary. To me, this means that *all* belief systems we construct are imaginary. It is only when we are inside the belief system, and it is cognitively and emotionally meaningful to us, that we cannot see that it is imaginary. If one of the imaginary realities we have constructed were the one, true world, we all would have found our way to it as we sought to explain things, as we eventually found our way to the double helix in biology and the laws of thermodynamics in physics. But that is not at all what has happened. Instead, we have created a fabulous array of imaginary realities in different cultures across history, each of them admirably creative, each

Figure 2.2 Prayer is a part of all the major religions, and it typically includes praying to supernatural beings for good favor. Here, two young Buddhist monks pray.

of them serving important psychological and social needs, but each of them most definitely imaginary.

Another criticism may be that science is my own god, and the scientific method my imaginary reality, and that in this sense my worldview is no different from, and no more valid than, the worldviews of those who believe in souls, shamans, and so on. To this I would say that the marvelous breakthrough of the scientific method is that it contains numerous safeguards against our tendencies for thinking in terms of imaginary realities. Its rules for what constitutes data, how a hypothesis can be tested, and what determines whether a conclusion is valid are designed to prevent us from bending reality into what we would prefer it to be. I will return to this issue at the end of the chapter.

The Psychological Origins of Imaginary Realities

It is not just in the misty human past that we can find the tendency to construct imaginary realities, nor is it just among unfamiliar peoples in remote parts of the world. Imaginary realities are here and now, in our daily lives, for all of us. We can see evidence of them in the development of children and in what adults today believe about how the world works.

Children's Imaginary Realities

Research on children's beliefs has included animism, anthropomorphism, magical thinking, teleology, and immanent justice.[2] Children's readiness to explain the world in terms of animism, anthropomorphism, and magical thinking can be seen in their fondness for stories that feature these themes. We read them stories about smiling suns, talking trees, and saying "Goodnight" to the moon, and they eagerly and credulously take part. Innumerable stories and cartoons feature animal characters in human roles, chattering away in the child's native language. Magic is also frequent in children's stories, and children eagerly embrace the reality of magical events. By telling and reading stories to children with these kinds of themes, adults play along, happy to promote the delusions their children clearly enjoy so much and charmed by children's ingenuous assumption that the stories are real.

Teleology also appears widely among children from an early age. To young children, everything has a purpose. Clouds are made to provide rain, some rocks are sharp so that animals have a place to scratch themselves, lions exist so that we can go to the zoo to see them. Many researchers and theorists on this topic conclude that this is where the belief in gods originates, in the teleological tendency to see everything as having been created intentionally, for a purpose.

The Expansion of Imaginary Realities in Adulthood

Researchers find that children grow out of many of their imaginary misunderstandings of the world in the course of middle childhood, beginning around age 6, and have mostly left them behind by age 11 or 12.[3] However, this finding is from research on people in countries where education is universal, including an education in basic scientific principles of how the natural world works. Ask yourself: How would an adult who had never been taught a scientific understanding of the world, who had never read a book about natural science (or any other book), whose only knowledge of the world came from local cultural beliefs—how would that person understand the world? After all, until about 200 years ago this description would apply to nearly all the adults who had ever lived. Such adults would, of course—any of us would, of course—believe what they had been taught, regardless of what they were taught, and their tendency for developing imaginary realities would be encouraged and elaborated, not thwarted, in the course of their early development. There would be no alternative way of understanding the world. As cultural animals, we have a strong psychological propensity for learning a cultural belief system and using it to interpret the world we live in and how to function in that world cognitively, emotionally, and socially.

But it is not just adults in the past who believed in a complex and intricate imaginary reality; adults today do so as well. Research indicates that immanent justice beliefs are even more common among adults than among children, indicating that adults teach children to think of the moral order in this way.[4] Many familiar religious and philosophical systems today include immanent justice, from the Eastern idea of karma to the Western concepts of heaven and hell. All carry the underlying theme that the universe has a moral order and that people ultimately get the fate they deserve. Irrespective of religious doctrines, researchers have found a widespread need among adults to believe in a "just world," that is, a world that has a moral order where good behavior is rewarded and bad behavior is punished, somehow. Similarly, it seems likely that beliefs in imaginary concepts such as souls, watchful ancestors, thought power, and the abilities of spiritual leaders have always been more common and entrenched among adults than among children, as these are beliefs that are acquired gradually through childhood and adolescence, reaching their mature form only in adulthood.

Current research indicates that adults' beliefs display many of the age-old tendencies to believe in imaginary realities. Magical thinking is common among adults, including the belief that you are what you eat, meaning that you may take on the traits of the animal you have for dinner, such as a boar (hairy) or a turtle (slow).[5] Across countries a majority of adults believe in a god and the efficacy of prayer. According to the Pew Research Center, about 40% of Americans believe in psychics and that "spiritual energy can be located in physical things."[6]

Astrology is one of the most widespread and enduring human beliefs. The prevalence of belief in astrology has actually grown in recent years and is stronger among younger Americans—the most educated generation in history—than among older Americans.[7] An international survey of adults in 21 countries found that from 45% to 90% believed it was "definitely" or "probably" true that "astrology—the study of star signs—has some scientific truth."[8] Belief in astrology is especially prevalent in India, the world's most populous country, where important life decisions such as marriage typically include consultation with an astrologer.

Why We Believe: The Psychological Origins of Imaginary Realities

What explains why we so easily embrace beliefs about the world that have no basis in fact? Here are some of the psychological principles involved.

Egocentrism: Making Gods in Our Image

There are many ways our psychology promotes the construction of imaginary realities. First and perhaps most obvious, imaginary realities are created by our egocentrism. We have a notable capacity for perspective-taking, but when we imagine other perspectives we often conflate them with our own. We know that we have goals, motives, and intentions and that other people do as well, so we assume that objects, animals, and natural forces have them, too.

There is also egocentrism in our creation of supernatural beings, who often turn out to be remarkably similar to us in their motivations and their emotional and social lives, and even in their physical appearance. In religious imagery, the gods of the Africans look like Africans, the gods of the Europeans look like Europeans, and the gods of the Asians look like Asians. The eternal soul is an egocentric creation; we have always experienced things, as far back as we can remember, so it is difficult for us to envision a future in which we would no longer be experiencing anything. Each of us constructs an individual identity in the course of childhood and adolescence, and it feels to us like "I" am something that is connected to the body but not synonymous with it. That is where the idea of the soul comes from.

Cognitive Errors: The Difficulty of Telling Correlation from Causation

Another major psychological contributor to our creation of imaginary realities is our tendency to confuse correlation with causation. In trying to make sense of the world around us, we frequently observe that one event took place before another event and conclude that the first event caused the second. Sometimes this is actually true. First the spring rains came; then the plants grew. First a man and a woman had sexual relations; then the woman became pregnant. However, we have a strong tendency to overextend this insight and misidentify all sorts of causation based only on correlation. First we prayed to the gods that the spring rains would come; then the spring rains came. First the woman performed a ritual to enhance fertility; then she became pregnant. First the shaman burned a sacrifice and rubbed the ashes on my father's abdomen where he was in pain; then his pain was relieved. First my neighbor looked at my daughter with the Evil Eye; then my daughter fell ill. In human thinking, without scientific training, everything is teleological. There are no accidents, no random events, no coincidences. Everything happens for a reason, and everything can be explained by psychological and social dynamics. Even people trained to think scientifically have to remind themselves constantly, and be reminded by others, that *correlation does not imply causation*.

One of the psychological quirks that makes this rule so hard to accept and remember is our tendency for *confirmation bias*, that is, the tendency to notice and recall the occasions when our expectations were confirmed and disregard the times we were wrong.[9] Remember how we prayed to the gods, but the spring rains didn't come? No, you probably don't. Or you excused it—perhaps we didn't pray hard enough, didn't offer the right sacrifice, or had not proved ourselves worthy of the rains. After the shaman's treatments, sometimes the person gets better and sometimes worse; if you believe in the shaman's power to heal, you are more likely to remember the times the person got better.

Intermittent reinforcement is another psychological principle that promotes confusion about correlation and causation. Decades ago, researchers working with rats discovered that the best way to get them to press a bar for a pellet reward was not to give them a reward every time, and not to give them a reward rarely, but to give them a reward intermittently—now and then. It works for humans, too. That is, we become more engaged and motivated for an activity when it provides rewards now and then. So, when we behave in ways inspired by our imaginary realities, the beliefs become all the more fervently held when they seem to produce occasional results. If you burn enough witches, every once in a while it results in the weather improving, a sick person getting better, or the cows producing more milk—or so it seems. When there is a correlation between the acts inspired by our imaginary realities and the outcomes we wished for, the power of intermittent reinforcement deepens our conviction that causation was involved.

The Need for Understanding and Control: Never Admit "I Don't Know"

Another contributor to our beliefs in imaginary realities is our psychological need to find an explanation for events rather than simply admitting that we have no idea why they happen. This tendency has been vividly demonstrated in research by neuroscientists Roger Sperry and Michael Gazzaniga. In the 1950s and 1960s one treatment for epilepsy was to cut the band of neural fibers, the corpus callosum, that connects the right and left hemispheres of the brain. This treatment was quite effective, but Sperry and Gazzaniga realized that it also provided an extraordinary experimental opportunity: you could present stimuli to one side of the brain but not the other, and only one half of the brain would be aware of it.

One of the most interesting findings from using this method was that when an image was presented to the nonverbal right half of the brain, and the person was asked to describe it, the verbal left half never simply responded "I don't know."[10] Instead, the person would make up an explanation. For example, when the command "Laugh" was shown to the right hemisphere, and people were then asked to explain why they started laughing, they would say something like "You guys are so funny!" This explanation-seeking, story-generating tendency of the left hemisphere is where the creation of imaginary realities originates in the brain.

The split-brain experiments show that it is essential, psychologically, for us to believe that important events happen for reasons we can explain. Finding—or inventing—an explanation for events confers a crucial sense of control. When things happen, especially unpleasant things, we find it intolerable to believe that there is nothing we can do about them. Creating control beliefs raises our spirits and gives us confidence that we are not helpless, that something can be done.

Many aspects of the imaginary realities we create have this need for control at their heart. For example, think of how important the weather has been throughout the history of humanity, the abrupt changes in heat and cold, the excess and then the absence of rain, the sudden natural disasters like hurricanes and earthquakes, and how baffling and befuddling these changes have been to the people experiencing them. It would have been deeply distressing to believe that something so vital was beyond our understanding and control, so we chose not to believe it. Recall from Chapter 1 that "weather control—attempted" is on the list of human cultural universals. We have similarly believed that we have control over illness and disease, over the growth of plants we rely on, and over the abundance of the animals we hunt, if we only pray to the right gods and perform the right magical rituals.

The belief that we can explain and control the important events around us helps give them meaning. We can endure suffering, and we have endured plenty of it throughout our species' history, and still do. But we can't endure *meaningless* suffering. Then we slide into despair. Our imaginary realities give our suffering meaning, and may even transform it into something we value, because we have endured it and prevailed. Our ability to ascribe meaning to our often chaotic, confusing experiences is crucial to our psychological survival, and imaginary realities are the key method we use to ascribe meaning. That is why we can't live without them.

Once we embrace an imaginary reality, it becomes the framework for making the world sensible and meaningful, and we hang on to it fiercely when challenged. This is the essence of cognitive dissonance, and although that term has become widely known and used, it is misleading. It is not the *cognitive* dissonance that matters; it is the dissonance that is *emotional* and *existential.* We grasp on to our imaginary realities as if our very lives depended on them, and in a way they do. This is why it is so difficult, close to impossible, to talk someone out of their belief in their imaginary reality, no matter how loony and unfounded it seems to you as someone who does not share it. You can make all the cognitive arguments you want, with the elegance and logic of a philosopher, and none of it will dent the emotional and existential commitment that protects the person's belief in their imaginary reality.

The Real Effects of the Imaginary

To complicate further the psychology of imaginary realities, sometimes our beliefs have real effects on our physical and psychological functioning that seem to validate our faith in them. The placebo effect has been well-established for over a century.[11] It shows that believing that you are taking a remedy for what ails you can actually have the medical, physiological consequences you expect. You'd still be better off with a surgeon than a shaman for that pain in your chest, but it is only we lucky humans living in recent times who have had access to such blessings. When the human psyche developed in our evolutionary history we had no recourse but our imagination, so we cleverly created beliefs that had at least some effect on relieving our physical and psychological suffering.

A related way that false beliefs have real effects is by reducing anxiety and stress. High levels of anxiety and stress have numerous negative effects on human functioning. They make it more difficult to focus on a task and apply our knowledge to it. They weaken us physiologically in the short term, and in the long term they damage our physical health. Hormones that are released when we experience high anxiety and stress, as part of the "fight-or-flight" response to threats, are helpful in the short term in preparing us to respond but harmful if they become chronic. Our imaginary realities help us reduce anxiety and stress by making threats seem comprehensible and controllable.[12] Imaginary reality beliefs won't make the rains come or the plague pass, but they may reduce anxiety and stress to manageable levels that will enable us to endure our crises and mobilize our full psychological resources to address them as best we can.

However, our beliefs in imaginary realities do not always promote our health, survival, and well-being. In fact, there is substantial evidence that what we believe can damage our health and even kill us. Anthropologists have reported from cultures in diverse parts of the world that people can die from believing they are cursed. Specifically, believing that someone with magical powers, usually a shaman, has directed deadly magic toward you can cause you to die. To observers, to the shamans, and to the doomed target of the curse as well, this seems like the ultimate proof that magic has real effects.

Imaginary Realities and the 4 Cs: Coordination, Cooperation, Cohesion, and Conformity

Among the Mbuti people of Central Africa, as reported by anthropologist Colin Turnbull in the mid-20th century, every hunting expedition begins with the Fire of the Hunt, a sacred campfire believed to guarantee the blessing of the forest and thereby bring good luck to the entire group for the day's hunt. After coming together for the Fire of the Hunt and singing songs appealing to the forest for hunting success, the group coordinates their hunting activities, with the men setting the nets and then the women and children beating the bushes and floor of the forest to drive the animals toward the nets.[13] In nearly every culture in the world you can find a similar example of shared beliefs as the basis for effective group cooperation.

All of the psychological reasons described so far for creating imaginary realities seem like errors and distortions that we commit in trying to make sense of things. That leaves us with a question: How did imaginary realities arise and survive evolutionary selection pressures if they represent such distortions of reality? As we have just seen, believing in imaginary realities has real positive effects on our individual psychological functioning. Additionally, imaginary realities have a variety of social benefits that enhance group survival. We can think of these as the 4 Cs: coordination, cooperation, cohesion, and conformity.

Émile Durkheim, the 19th-century French sociologist, was the first to recognize the value of imaginary realities for promoting the 4 Cs. Durkheim focused on religious rituals in tribal societies and portrayed them as a valuable source of group cohesion. Rituals and ceremonies exist in all human societies to deepen group adherence to supernatural beliefs and the rules and expectations they represent. By presenting the rules of cooperation and coordination as established by supernatural forces, cultural groups give those rules much greater psychological and social power, enhancing group cohesion. Shared beliefs in supernatural forces also make it more likely that people will adhere to group rules, because they are kept in line not only by social monitoring from others in their group but by monitoring (and potential punishment) from supernatural forces.[14]

More recent theorists have echoed Durkheim and added an evolutionary twist.[15] In the current view, as for Durkheim, shared beliefs in supernatural powers promote group cooperation, coordination, and cohesion. In the course of human evolutionary history, groups who possessed shared beliefs thus had an advantage over competing hominin groups. Consequently, the tendency to embrace shared beliefs in supernatural powers prevailed and is today a near-universal feature of our imaginary realities.

Research in developmental psychology has provided insights into how shared beliefs develop.[16] The process begins in infancy, with babies' eagerness for *joint attention* with those who care for them, which means two people focusing attention on the same object or action. From the early months babies direct their attention to whatever their caregiver is looking at, and as they develop abilities to vocalize and gesture they seek to gain their caregiver's attention to the object of their interest. Joint attention soon develops into *shared intentionality*, which entails two or more people coordinating their intentions toward a common goal. Our innate tendencies for developing shared intentionality provide a fertile foundation for learning shared beliefs about imaginary realities.

The Missing (but Crucial) C: Conformity

Descriptions of the human tendencies for cooperation, coordination, and cohesion may make it seem that we typically form imaginary realities as equals, collaboratively. Cooperation, coordination, and cohesion all seem on the face of it to be social processes that take place voluntarily. We begin with shared intentionality as children and develop that collaboration into shared beliefs. I think there is some truth to this, in the sense that we possess various psychological tendencies that dispose us toward these 3 Cs. However, there is a crucial 4th C that this formulation does not acknowledge: conformity. As we grow up in a human culture, it is true that we look for ways to coordinate and cooperate with others, including coordinating our beliefs. But in most cultures we are not offered a range of possible imaginary realities and invited to choose among them. On the contrary, we are fully expected to conform to the conceptions of imaginary realities that are believed by others in our culture and taught to us implicitly and explicitly as we grow up. The social costs of questioning or rejecting the imaginary realities of our culture are typically harsh and painful: gossip, hostility, shaming, and even ostracism.

One key to conformity, and by extension to cultural learning of imaginary realities, is our strong propensity for imitation. This shows up even in the early weeks of life. Joint attention is a form of imitation: I notice you are looking at something, and then I look at it, too. Language learning includes a substantial amount of imitation, and it begins in the preverbal, often imitative social exchanges between babies and those who care for them. Even as early as the second year of life, children imitate peers as a way of breaking the ice socially and implicitly opening the door to social bonds. As children develop they increasingly imitate peers and adults, especially the ones who are perceived as high in status. Much of children's play with peers, friends, and siblings involves imitation, for example, in pretend play where children take on imaginary roles. Other apes engage in some degree of imitation, too, but not as much as we do even at age two, and with each year the gap between us and apes in imitative tendencies grows wider.[17] It is easy to see how our tendency for imitation could be extended to imitating others' beliefs about imaginary realities.

Imitation is a key part of our tendency to learn and adhere to *social norms*, the typical patterns of thought and behavior expected in a social group or culture. Our responsiveness to social norms is, in turn, a key to the development of imaginary realities, because it includes a readiness to distort perceptions of physical reality in favor of shared beliefs. For example, in one famous study four-year-olds were shown pictures of two elephants, one clearly larger than the other. By themselves, they could easily identify which was largest. However, when grouped with three other children who had been instructed by the experimenter to state that the smaller elephant was in fact larger, children readily conformed to the group consensus despite their awareness that it was wrong. Similar studies demonstrating conformity have been done for decades with adults.[18] In this we can see the developmental origins of a broader readiness to accept a cultural imaginary reality over a physical reality. When cultural beliefs collide with physical perceptions, cultural beliefs prevail.

Conformity is an essential ingredient for understanding how tendencies for imitation and adherence to social norms become shared beliefs in imaginary realities. We are inherently social, and we have strong tendencies for the other Cs, but the tendency for conformity makes the development of shared beliefs a top-down process, not a collaboration among equals. Hierarchy, rank, prestige, and power are always part of human relations, and part of social relations among our closest ape relatives, too, indicating that these features go deep into our psychological nature. In most cultures, age is a key marker of power, with older people having power over younger people, at least until old age, when power often diminishes. Thus, older siblings, parents, grandparents, and other older persons ensure that children conform to beliefs in the imaginary reality that prevails in their culture.

Because of our psychological nature as cultural animals, and our vulnerability and dependence during a long childhood, we readily accept the hierarchy of age, and we readily conform to the way of life our siblings, parents, grandparents, other relatives, neighbors, and community members model for us and sometimes teach us directly, including the imaginary realities that are the basis of their understanding of the world. If we resist or reject what we are taught, we are subject to social and physical punishments that show us the formidable costs of disobedience. But typically we readily accept these imaginary realities as true portrayals of the life around us, no more subject to doubt than our status as brother or sister, child and grandchild. Research shows that children not only swiftly accept rules and norms; they enforce them on their peers and become irate when their peers violate them.[19]

When we reach puberty, traditionally in most cultures there is a ritual process that entails even more explicit and intensive teaching of imaginary realities, often accompanied by seclusion and sometimes by physical and psychological trials.[20] The Catholic confirmation ritual and the Jewish bar and bat mitzvah are vestiges of these traditional rituals that persist today, but they are far milder than the puberty rituals in most cultures that have been described by anthropologists. The rituals for boys frequently have involved sleep deprivation and the infliction of pain and fear. After we come through these puberty rituals we are considered ready—socially and ideologically—to move toward full adult status and responsibilities. The stress and pain the rituals often entail have the psychological effect of binding us all the more strongly to the worldview of the group (Figure 2.3).

But we eventually become capable of critical thinking as adults, which allows us to question the precepts we were taught by our elders when we were young and decide what we really believe. Right? Well, this was the conventional wisdom in psychology for many decades, but it was based on a very limited cultural-historical slice of humanity, those living in democratic Western countries during the late 20th century. In that cultural-historical context, that was the ideal: to grow up to become an individualistic, independent person, capable of thinking critically about all you had been taught and then deciding for yourself what your view of the world would be.

But this is not at all how humans have developed in our species' history. Children were not presented with a variety of beliefs about the world in the course of their childhood education and invited to choose among them. There was no exposure to diverse ways of thinking among diverse peoples. There was only the imaginary reality that everyone in your culture believed and taught you from babyhood onward, in direct and indirect ways.

Figure 2.3 Across cultures, puberty rituals are a common way of deepening commitment to cultural beliefs. Here is a group of boys of the Maasai culture in Tanzania, shortly after passing through the public circumcision ritual required for boys to qualify for manhood.

Of course you believed it, as everyone else did. It never occurred to you to believe otherwise. How could it, when no alternative worldview was available? Being born a cultural animal, ready and eager to embrace the ways of the people around you, you accepted the imaginary reality presented to you, and it never even occurred to you that it was imaginary. As you knew it, it was only the world-as-it-is.

Conform or Else

The pyramids of Egypt, built about 4,500 years ago, seem even now like astounding feats of engineering and cultural cooperation. The largest of them, the Great Pyramid of Giza (Figure 2.4), towers 481 feet above the ground and is made of an estimated 2.3 million stone blocks, each weighing from 2.5 to 15 tons, transported from hundreds of miles away (that is, dragged across the desert somehow; this was before wheels were invented). Each of the three Giza pyramids was part of a large complex of buildings, including palace temples and temporary cities inhabited by thousands of laborers recruited (that is, enslaved) from far and wide to build the pyramids. Thousands of other people served on the project as organizers, managers, scribes, and artists. The pyramids were the tombs of the pharaohs and contained all the goods and provisions the pharaoh would need in the afterlife, but they also contained many elaborate drawings of wide-ranging scenes of Egyptian life, along with inscriptions and texts on religious rituals and burial practices as well as mundane aspects of everyday life: farming and fishing, animal care, carpentry, leisure, and so on.

We can all marvel now at this tremendous achievement of Egyptian civilization, but for anyone curious about the psychology of human nature, the

Figure 2.4 The Great Pyramid of Giza. Stairway to heaven?

question to be answered is *Why?* No other animal would expend such a massive amount of labor and resources on something with a dubious relation to survival and reproduction, so why did we? The answer seems pretty simple at first: because the pharaoh wanted it so. But there is a deeper psychological truth that this implies: because when we believe in an imaginary reality, we will do almost anything in service of it.

There is an additional psychological truth as a corollary: because we are psychologically prone to conformity within an established social hierarchy, and when a person in power decrees that something will be done, we usually fall into line. A feat like the Egyptian pyramids requires an impressive degree of cooperation, coordination, and cohesion, that is true, but above all it requires conformity. Often we are not given much choice. The consequences of refusing to conform to the cultural hierarchy have frequently been dire, even fatal. But we usually conform without much resistance, doing our best to survive the life we find ourselves in.

Frequently in human societies, powerful persons can determine the direction of a whole society based on their personal inspirations of imaginary realities. The pharaoh decides he wants a monstrously large tomb to ease his entry to the afterlife, and for decades an entire society is devoted to building it. It helps that all the people whose conformity is required for the project have also been taught this imaginary reality, including the supernatural worthiness of the pharaoh to whom the entire gargantuan enterprise is dedicated.

The Imaginary, the Psychotic, and the Fictional

It is easy for us to see from a modern perspective that the entire vast project of the building of the pyramids was based on an imaginary reality. After death the pharaoh did not find himself in paradise accompanied by all the luxury goods buried along with him—we are pretty sure of that now. As usual, it is easy for anyone outside an imaginary reality to see that it is false.

If a national leader today announced a vast, multidecade, astoundingly expensive project to build a tomb laden with riches to ease the leader's transition to an afterlife paradise, the rest of the world would surely respond with horror and incredulity. We would assume the leader is a deluded egomaniac, at best, and probably mentally ill. This raises a key question for our discussion of imaginary realities: What separates believing in an imaginary reality from being psychotic? Delusions, false beliefs, are a hallmark symptom of psychosis, but the argument of this chapter and this book is that we all have delusions, that humans are inherently prone to false beliefs in imaginary realities. Where is the line between the imaginary realities we all have and the delusions that people have only when they are mentally ill?

It is not really a line; it is more like a wide gray border that shifts with historical time and cultural context. Imaginary realities are culturally acceptable and approved and are built out of culturally available ideas. People can hold beliefs in imaginary realities and still function productively in their culture. In fact, belief in a shared imaginary reality enhances functioning in everyday life, because it reduces anxiety and stress and promotes cooperation, coordination, cohesion, and conformity. The delusions that occur in psychosis, by contrast, are lonely delusions. Only the afflicted person holds them; other people in the culture, even those closest to them, find their beliefs alarming and disturbing, as they are clearly out of touch with the world-as-it-is.

A related issue concerns the boundary between imaginary realities and fictional worlds.[21] By "fictional worlds" I mean worlds we know to be invented but still enjoy taking part in, through oral stories, plays, games, poems, novels and short stories, songs, paintings and sculptures, and other forms of artistic expression. Our love of fictional worlds is a reflection of our capacity for creating and believing in imaginary realities. Fictional worlds are a form of play that utilizes this capacity. We know fictional worlds are not real, but we have the capacity to enter them temporarily, to "suspend our disbelief" and be emotionally, cognitively, and socially affected by them *as if* they were true. Who has not had the experience of entering a fictional world and being deeply affected by it, caring earnestly about the anguish, pain, and triumphs of characters who do not actually exist?

It is only in recent human history that a distinction has been established between imaginary realities and fictional worlds. Virtually all cultures studied by anthropologists and all cultures in the past that have left written records have stories of imaginary realities that explain how their people came to be and the divinely established nature of their relations to others within the group, to other human groups, to the natural world, and to supernatural forces. However, people within a culture typically regard their cultural stories not as fictions but as The One True World, and throughout human history they have often been willing to kill or die in conflicts with other groups in order to defend the validity of their culture's imaginary reality. Only in the past several hundred years, and especially in the past century, have societies become literate enough and artistic production become abundant enough for most people in most places also to have access to stories they acknowledge as fictional but enjoy as a form of play.

Nevertheless, the literal truth of imaginary realities remains contested in many places, particularly in the realm of religion. Within many of the major religions, fierce disagreements and conflicts occur between "progressivist" adherents, who regard their religion's doctrines as meaningful stories but not to be taken literally, and "fundamentalists," who vigorously defend the literal truth of their religion's doctrines and tales of religious heroes.[22] Implicitly at stake in these conflicts is the psychological power of the doctrine, because imaginary realities lose much of their psychological power once they are recognized as being imaginary.

The Brilliance of the Imaginary

We are a species that is full of delusions. Our false beliefs about how the world works and our place in it are a fundamental part of our psychology. No matter when or where we live, we never take the reality of our situation as it is and look at it straight on. Instead, we embellish it, reshape it, and transform it into something understandable and controllable. It is not that we always believe that the world we live in is ultimately benevolent and always results in happy endings. On the contrary, we are as likely to imagine demons and black magic as to imagine friendly spirits and good omens. But our imaginary realities always transform reality into something different than it actually is, so that we can comprehend it and believe we at least partially control it.

Does this tendency to create imaginary realities make us a ridiculous and pathetic species? Certainly we often see the imaginary realities held by people in other cultures as ridiculous and pathetic. From the outside looking in, it is painfully obvious that the realities they live by, the ultimate sources of meaning in their life, are imaginary. But does that mean *all* imaginary realities must be admitted to be desperate fabrications, the inventions of a species that can't handle the harshness of real life?

I would prefer to respond to this with a sympathetic acknowledgment of the human condition. It is difficult to be a species with such an immense talent for imagining potential threats. That is a highly useful ability, because it enables us to avoid many of the threats we anticipate. But it is psychologically taxing, too, because we are continually imagining threats that never appear. Creating imaginary realities allows us to place all those threats into a system that we can understand and potentially control. Even if that sense of understanding and control is illusory, it quells our fears and gives us the confidence and psychological strength to act effectively in a world that is mostly beyond our comprehension.

Keep in mind, too, how much suffering, pain, and death people have been required to confront in the course of a typical lifetime through nearly all of human history. Living now in an era when people in nearly all countries have a life expectancy of at least 70 years and rates of infant and child mortality are at an all-time low, it is difficult for us to grasp the grim human reality that our ancestors had to bear. For almost all of them, suffering, pain, and death were ubiquitous. If they lived to adulthood, nearly all of them witnessed the early death of people they loved—children, siblings, parents, cousins, aunts, uncles, friends. They felt the grief, the longing, the disorienting and overwhelming conviction that *this cannot be true*, even as their loved ones kept appearing in their thoughts and dreams, their presence agonizingly real. Who could blame them for inventing imaginary realities that would make that reality less harsh?

With no scientific knowledge, our ancestors found many events terrifying and mystifying. Weather patterns would suddenly change, food sources that seemed abundant would disappear, their apparently healthy loved ones would suddenly get sick and die, their own feelings of robust health would abruptly turn to pain, discomfort, and weakness. As an inquisitive animal with a strong predisposition against admitting "I don't know" to the question of why events occur, we needed compelling stories to explain these phenomena, so we invented them.

You could see the invention of our imaginary realities as a ridiculous and pathetic response to a mystifying world, but you could also see it as brilliant and worth celebrating. Somehow we learned to transform our harsh and painful reality into something we could handle, and sometimes even into something glorious, something that would inspire consolation and hope. Think, for example, of the Africans abducted and transported hundreds of years ago across the ocean to be made slaves in America, a place where they had no freedom and knew nothing, not even the local language. In these desperate circumstances, many of them embraced the imaginary reality of the ancient Hebrew stories, of the Jews as slaves under Pharaoh, and believed that they, too, would eventually be liberated—if not in this life, then in the afterlife, together with God for eternity. Here is an example of a "spiritual" they created and sang in the 19th century with this theme, of gazing like Moses over the Jordan River to the Promised Land—Israel, for Moses; heaven, for the slaves.

> Deep river
> My home is over Jordan
> Deep river
> I want to cross over into campground
> Oh don't you want to go home
> To that Promised Land
> That Promised Land
> Where all is peace
> Deep river, Lord
> I want to cross over into campground

Their imaginary reality made it possible for them not just to survive but to find occasional joy in a world that, in its raw, untransformed condition, offered little of it. Even today an African American church is one of the most joyful and hopeful places you will ever find.

Imaginary Realities in the Scientific Era

Beginning about 400 years ago, humans invented a new approach to understanding the world: the scientific method. This invention has dramatically transformed human life and is rapidly transforming the entire planet in our time. No longer is it believed that human physiological functioning is based on the balance of four "humors"—blood, phlegm, yellow bile, and black bile—now that the scientific method has revealed this belief to be something Hippocrates pulled out of his ear 2,500 years ago, an imaginary physiology if you will. No longer is it believed that illnesses result from "miasmas" or "bad air," now that science has shown their true sources are viruses and bacteria that cannot be seen with the naked eye. No longer is it believed that the earth is flat or that the sun, moon, and stars revolve around the earth, now that science has revealed that it is we on earth who are revolving around the sun, which is part of a vast galaxy of other suns, which is only one of a mind-boggling array of other galaxies.

Do the remarkable and continuous advances in knowledge that are yielded by the scientific method mean that one day soon we will no longer be in need of imaginary realities? Certainly there is less suffering today in the typical human life than there once was, and the suffering that still occurs is mostly explainable by scientific principles rather than by imaginary concepts. Most people today who have received at least a basic education accept most of the scientific realities about the world.

Nevertheless, the psychology of human nature, formed over hundreds of thousands of years of our genetic and cultural evolution, has not changed, and that psychology includes a strong predisposition to create imaginary realities.[23] It is possible for us to think scientifically, but it is always an effort. So many of our natural psychological tendencies conspire against it. We can learn the principles of the scientific method and the basic scientific information about the physical world, while still maintaining many of our beliefs about imaginary realities.[24] Many people, including eminent scientists, manage to accept that the universe is billions of years old and that life on earth evolved from microbes and that humans evolved from other primates over millions of years, and yet also believe a religious faith that maintains that everything in the physical world was created in more or less its current form by a formidable human-like "father" god a few thousand years ago. The Chinese government has been vigorously attempting to stamp out all supernatural beliefs since communism was established in the mid-20th century, yet even now there is no place like China for diversity in methods of enhancing the likelihood of "good luck." During the COVID-19 pandemic that began in 2020, religious fervor surged all over the world, in relatively devout and relatively secular countries alike, as people resorted to prayer and traditional rituals in an attempt to control and prevent a disease that was rapidly spreading debility and death. The internet, which is among the most advanced scientific and technological achievements of all time, is rife with imaginary realities based on extreme political and religious views.

Some years ago I interviewed emerging adults in Denmark about their religious beliefs.[25] Given that Denmark is renowned as the least religious country in the world, I was curious as to what young Danes would believe about what happens when we die—if anything. Although none of them believed in a traditional religious doctrine, most of them believed that existence continues in some form after death. "I've chosen to believe in something [after death], because I can't tolerate the idea that if someone in your family dies, there's nothing more," said one young woman. "Our soul can't just disappear," said another. "It lives on, in one place or another." A frequently used phrase was "There's more between heaven and earth," to imply the possibility of an imaginary reality and the limits of human knowledge. One young man, considering the possibility of life after death, said, "I'm not sure what I believe, but there's more between heaven and earth. Just because we can't prove something doesn't mean it doesn't exist."

It is true that, according to cross-national research today, people in the poorest and most unstable countries are the most likely to hold religious beliefs. People in countries where access to scientifically based medical care is limited are the most likely to believe in magical cures for illnesses. Those in countries where people receive the least education are the most likely to believe in imaginary phenomena like witches and astrology. However, even in countries with the highest physical and economic security, imaginary realities persist. Even in Denmark, an affluent and smoothly functioning society that ranks highest in the world in happiness in international surveys, imaginary realities can still be a source of the 4 Cs and can still provide consolation and meaning for suffering and death. Wherever we live, we still suffer pain and disappointment, we still grieve for our loved ones who die, and we still face death ourselves. And of course we all still maintain our individual imaginary realities, no matter when and where we live. It is how we are made.

3
Anxiety-Prone Threat Detectors
Why We Imagine the World as Full of Threats

Not long ago, an internet advice column featured a letter from a mother who was worried about her 13-year-old son. The boy had seen an internet headline, "World War 3: How Helsinki Is Preparing for War with Russia," and was now deeply concerned that war might occur and inflame the entire planet. "He really felt like the world as he knows it could come to an end, and it really scared him," lamented his mother. "How can I be reassuring without overloading him?" She signed the letter, "Terrified Mom." The advice columnist assured the mother that her concerns were not overblown or misplaced. "This is a completely awful time to raise kids," the columnist intoned. "Children live with the fear of nuclear annihilation, planetary destruction, flood, famine, fire, mass shootings, and civil war. It is, to put it plainly, fucking awful."[1]

For anyone seeking to understand imaginary realities, this is, in many respects, a remarkable exchange. From a factual, statistical, historical perspective, there has never been a better, safer, more abundant time to raise children—or to be alive as an adult—than right now.[2] Throughout human history, until the invention of vaccines and antibiotics in recent times, children were highly vulnerable to disease, and they often died in infancy or early childhood. The total human population remained stable for thousands of years until a few centuries ago, which means that women typically gave birth to up to 8 or 10 children in the course of their reproductive lives (if they lived through all those pregnancies and births), yet only two or three of those children would survive to adulthood. Food was scarce, and children often went hungry or ate barely enough to survive, as did their parents. In most cultures children's disobedience or errors were punished with a smack, a whipping, or a beating, their parents believing corporal punishment was not only acceptable but necessary for children to learn how to behave properly. Children usually started contributing important work to their family by middle childhood, and many cultures had a custom of sending children

Imaginary Realities. Jeffrey Jensen Arnett, Oxford University Press. © Jeffrey Jensen Arnett (2026).
DOI: 10.1093/9780197817407.003.0003

out to work for another family in exchange for a meager payment to the parents. Girls were often married off shortly after they reached puberty, in an arrangement made by their family without their own involvement or consent. Very few children attended school, and nearly all of them were illiterate, as the adults were.

None of these dire realities is still prevalent. Infant and child mortality are far lower now than they have ever been in human history, worldwide. Revolutions in food production have made adequate nourishment available for nearly all the 8 billion humans who now populate the earth. Corporal punishment is disapproved and even illegal in much of the world (although it still exists in many places). Likewise, child labor is illegal in most of the world, although it still takes place. Most children spend most of their childhood years going to school, although access to education beyond primary school varies widely among nations. In all of these ways, you would have to conclude that there has never been a better time to be a child or raise a child, in the entire history of humanity.

Yet the fears of "Terrified Mom" and the columnist lamenting our "f***ing awful" times are real and should not be scoffed at or waved away. There are billions of people who feel as they do, that the world is full of perils and that this is an especially threatening and disturbing time to be alive, for children and adults alike. Why? What are the psychological motives that lead us to construct imaginary realities that make us fearful, anxious, and stressed even when our objective reality is in many ways favorable?

These are the questions we will take on in this chapter. Let's start with an examination of the psychological origins of anxiety. Then we will look at some of the specific sources of stress in our time, in particular the jarring mismatch between our psychological tendencies and the barrage of inflammatory electronic information each of us is subjected to on a daily basis. Finally, we will explore the benefits of anxiety and stress, including how we really would not want to live without them.

Small and Vulnerable for Years: The Original Source of Anxiety

We have a lot of company among other animals in our experience of anxiety. The physiological and behavioral signs of anxiety are highly similar across species: accelerated heart rate, perspiration, secretion of stress hormones, restlessness, heightened vigilance, and decreased feeding and exploratory behavior. Anxiety is widespread for a simple but powerful reason: it is essential to survival, especially when we are young. Being anxiety-prone makes you a good threat detector.

Nearly all animals face threats to their survival and well-being on a daily basis, from predators or from competitors within their own species. If you are provoked to anxiety when cues to possible threats appear, you are more likely to be prepared to evade them. It is an advantage to be relatively easily provoked to anxiety, because then you will not miss any genuine threats. True, you may often experience distress unnecessarily, when it turns out the threat was not genuine after all, but your distress is of little consequence from an evolutionary perspective. It is far better for you, survival-wise, to experience anxiety 99 times when there was no real threat in order to detect the 100th time when the threat was genuine, rather than to be blissfully unaware of any threat the first 99 times only to fall victim to it the 100th time. The tiger you believe you hear rustling in the grass, about to pounce on you, may turn out to be only the wind nearly every time, but you sure don't want to mistake that rustling for the wind the one time it turns out to be a tiger.

This useful tendency to be easily provoked to anxiety is part of what social psychologist Paul Rozin calls the *negativity bias*, which he defines as our tendency to find negative events and experiences more noticeable and psychologically powerful than positive ones.[3] For example, with us as with other animals, one unpleasant digestive response to a particular food can result in a deep and lasting aversion to that food, a phenomenon called *conditioned taste aversion*. There is no positive experience with food that has such an enduring effect. Similarly, phobias, which are extreme anxieties in response to one particular kind of stimulus, can also be deeply ingrained as a consequence of one negative experience. One traumatic experience with a dog can make you deeply anxious in the presence of all dogs for a long time to come, maybe for all time. Seen in this light, our frequent experience of anxiety, even though it is usually unwarranted, is not a defect in our psychological system; it is how we and numerous other creatures evolved, with good reason.

We can see the value of anxiety clearly by focusing on our early experience of it when we are young and most vulnerable. Our first experience of anxiety is *stranger anxiety*, the fear of unfamiliar persons that begins to develop when babies are about six months old.[4] There is an evolutionary basis for our development of stranger anxiety at this age. This is the time when infants first become mobile, and learning to crawl allows them to begin to explore the environment but also carries the risk that they may crawl themselves into big trouble. Learning to stay close to familiar persons and avoid unfamiliar persons and places helps infants stay near those who will protect them and keep them safe. Stranger anxiety peaks when children begin to walk, at about 12 to 18 months of age across cultures. Once they are able to walk, children are even more vulnerable because they can find trouble—and danger—even faster than before. So it makes sense that we would be evolutionarily prepared to be fearful of strange people and strange situations, especially at this stage of life.

It is an evolutionary advantage to be reflexively anxious in response to people and situations that are unfamiliar, but of course it is also important for us to explore the world and learn more about it from an early age so that we can develop the skills to live in it successfully. Consequently, under normal conditions young children use familiar persons as a *secure base* from which to explore the surrounding environment. If a threat appears in the environment, anxiety is activated and children seek direct physical contact with familiar, loving persons who can be relied upon to protect them. Once the threat recedes, children resume their exploratory activities.

Because we are cultural animals and must learn the ways and skills of our culture rather than relying on instincts, we are more vulnerable, for longer, than any other species. After the peak at 12 to 18 months of age, as children come to know more about the world and become more capable of judging which persons and situations represent serious threats, their stranger anxiety wanes, but very gradually. It does not really disappear until they approach adulthood, because they remain vulnerable until then, and it is worthwhile to remain wary of the unknown.

We Do Believe in Spooks: Imaginary Threats as Sources of Anxiety

The anxiety we experience in response to strangers and the unfamiliar as infants and toddlers is highly similar to the anxiety other animals experience when they are young and small, and for similar and obvious reasons of needing to be protected from threats in the environment. However, beyond these early years new sources of anxiety develop in us that are more distinctively human. Beginning when we are three or four years old and continuing throughout our life, our most important, frequent, and formidable sources of anxiety are not the ones we see right in front of us but the ones we imagine, the ones that we conjure up in our heads.

Not all our early fears are imaginary. Fear of animals and fear of the dark are two of the top anxieties of childhood.[5] Both of these make good evolutionary sense, so it is not surprising we are prepared to learn them. Animals have preyed on us at various times in our evolutionary history. We are a beast that relies a lot on sight, and our sense of smell is a lot less powerful than in most other mammals, so when it is dark we are quite vulnerable. We are especially vulnerable when we are in the dark and alone, so it is not surprising that children often resist sleeping in a separate room by themselves. In most of the world, throughout human history and even now, young children have slept alongside their parents. In some affluent, individualistic societies today, parents have their own bedroom and children are supposed to sleep separately from infancy onward, in another bed and another room so that parents can have their couple privacy and their marital intimacy. But children often disrupt this plan in early childhood by striving intensely to join their parents.

In addition to their reasonable fears of animals and the dark, young children often fear imaginary creatures: ghosts and monsters, "bad guys," devils and demons, or whatever fearful images their culture has created and taught them. Adults often use children's readiness for imagining fearful creatures to intimidate and control them, warning them that if they don't behave The Monster will come and take them away and the parents will do nothing to stand in its way.

We do not stop responding with anxiety to imaginary threats once we reach adulthood. On the contrary, our anxieties multiply as our imaginations become more powerful and complex. As we learn the imaginary realities that are dominant in our culture, those beliefs give form to our anxieties. It's not just children who believe in ghosts and monsters, devils and demons; it's adults, too, in most times and places. Nor are these beliefs solely a relic of our ignorant past or confined to places where people receive little education and superstitions thrive. In recent national surveys, about half of Americans said they believe in ghosts and demons.[6] In a separate national survey, 61% of Americans said they believe in the devil (Figure 3.1).[7]

It is easy to see the evolutionary survival value of being anxiety-prone in response to fierce animals or dark places, but why do we so readily believe in threatening imaginary beings like ghosts and demons? One explanation is that these are manifestations of our conscience and so serve the function

Figure 3.1 The Devil has appeared frequently in the history of Western art and literature, typically with horns and wings. This is a drawing by Baccio Baldini from the 15th century in Italy.

of restraining our self-interest and keeping us in line with cultural expectations for behavior. Often the threatening beings have a moral quality. They don't just attack or menace randomly; they are unleashed when you have done something wrong or are tempted to do so. Or the god or God or angels or ancestors whose function is to protect you from malevolent forces will protect you only if you stay in line and believe and do as you are told. It may be that we developed a readiness to embrace these kinds of beliefs because doing so promotes conformity to social rules and norms, even if it does so at the cost of widespread anxiety.

The Costs and Benefits of Fearing the Future

To a large extent, our pervasive anxiety is a consequence of our extraordinary ability to imagine and anticipate the future. Other animals experience fear when there is a direct threat in the environment, and they experience anxiety if there is some sign or cue that a direct threat is about to appear, but no other animal has the capacity for anticipating future events the way we do. One of the most important and useful qualities of the prefrontal cortex is that it gives us the ability to anticipate threats and act to avoid them before they appear. But the cost of that ability is that we experience anxiety over many things that never happen and over some things that never had more than a very slight chance of happening.

You can see that consequence today in surveys about what causes people anxiety. If Americans' anxieties were based on what is statistically most likely to threaten our health and our lives, we would be most fearful of obesity, because it is a strong risk factor for all the top sources of mortality: heart disease, stroke, diabetes, and cancer. We would also be anxious every time we get into a car, because for Americans under age 45 automobile accidents are the most common cause of death, and auto accidents continue to be a major cause of death through old age. But most of us are not anxious about obesity and automobiles. Those don't even show up on long lists of things Americans fear most.[8]

So what do we actually fear? What are our main sources of anxiety? Some of our fears are quite reasonable. About half of us fear not having enough money for the future. This sensible fear may have the beneficial effect of making us set money aside when we can, in order to be prepared for difficult economic times when they come. So in this case our ability to anticipate the future is constructive and rational. About a third of us fear reptiles and a quarter of us fear insects and spiders. Although few of us are in peril from these threats today, it is clear that it would have been evolutionarily useful for us to develop a tendency to fear them in the human past.

We also fear many things that have only a low probability of occurring. Near the top of the list in surveys of Americans' most potent anxieties are terrorist attacks and mass shootings, feared by about half of adults. These events are shocking, horrifying, and spectacular when they occur, but the chance that any American will be a victim of such events is vanishingly small. Even in our exceptionally violent country, we are more likely to die from a lightning strike or a bathtub accident than from either a terrorist attack or a mass shooting. Similarly, over one-fifth of Americans fear natural disasters such as hurricanes, floods, droughts, and earthquakes. These, too, are spectacularly harmful but rare events. Worldwide, the pattern of perceived threats is similar. In a survey of 28 countries in various world regions, at least half of those surveyed perceived threats from terrorist attacks, natural disasters, and nuclear or chemical warfare.[9]

Yet even if a threat has a low probability of occurring, it might make sense to take steps to avoid it, so long as the cost of those steps is not too high. This is especially true if the consequences of the threat would be devastating. A case in point is fear of a pandemic. A few years ago, this fear might have seemed overblown. It had been nearly a century since a major infectious disease had spread worldwide, the flu pandemic of 1918–1920. It may have seemed to many that the days of worldwide pandemics were past and that it was not worth expending current resources to prepare for them. Now we know better. The COVID-19 pandemic that began in 2020 has killed more than 7 million people globally, and over 800 million people have been infected. The consequences would have been even deadlier if it had spread unchecked, but the invention of effective vaccines in record time, made possible by a worldwide health research infrastructure that was built for exactly this kind of rare but devastating threat, kept it from becoming even worse than it was.

Today we have scientific institutions to help quell our fears about damaging events, but those institutions were established only recently. In the past we did not have science, but we hated feeling helpless about threats, so we invented superstitions to give us a sense of control.[10] Superstitions adhere especially to momentous and potentially perilous events like childbirth. Because our big brains make for big heads, childbirth is more painful and dangerous for us than for any other species. The longer the labor, the more exhausted the mother and the greater the potential danger to mother and child. Consequently, cultures have created a wide variety of practices intended to speed labor along.[11] The most widespread approach, appearing in cultures in all parts of the world, is to use some kind of imagery or metaphor associated with opening up or expulsion. For example, in the Philippines a key (for "opening" the cervix) and a comb (for "untangling" the umbilical cord) are placed under the laboring woman's pillow. In other cultures, ropes are unknotted, bottles are uncorked, or animals are let out of their pens. In some traditional cultures, the midwife calls on spiritual assistance from a shaman. According to traditional beliefs among the Kuna Indians of Central America, for example, difficult births are caused by the spirit of the womb, Muu, who may decide for inscrutable reasons to hold on to the fetus and prevent it from coming out. The shaman's job is to invoke magic that will release the fetus from Muu's grip, by singing a song that sends a spirit inside the womb to wage combat against Muu.

The many superstitions surrounding childbirth provide another clue to the function that superstitions serve. They do not have any direct effect on events that occur, but they may enable us to ease our anxiety in tense, stressful situations. Furthermore, following them may have indirect consequences, because the belief may have the real effect of easing anxiety. If you are a pregnant woman and embrace the various birth superstitions of your culture, it may ease your fears and give you more confidence as the birth approaches, with real positive consequences for the subsequent experience of childbirth. If you believe birth rituals will ease your pain, they really may ease your pain due to the placebo effect.

However, not all superstitions have such salutary effects. It is hard to see the usefulness of fearing black cats or avoiding "unlucky" numbers or believing that evil creatures come out during a full moon. Just about every culture has a wide range of superstitions among its cultural beliefs that require changes in behavior and that evoke anxiety when they are violated, to no apparent purpose.[12] If you are Chinese, avoid the number 4 because of its phonetic resemblance to the word for "death." Similarly, if you are Japanese, avoid sticking your chopsticks into your rice straight up, because in that form they resemble the character for the number 4, whose sound resembles the word for "death" in Japanese, too. In some parts of India, it is considered bad luck to get your hair cut on a Tuesday. Many cultures associate certain animals with evil or bad luck—black cats in the West, crows in Korea. Egyptians traditionally believed that if you see or hear an owl, that means bad news is on the way. Many of these superstitions result from our tendency to confuse correlation with causation. Sometimes after you see or hear an owl you really do receive bad news. If you already believed the owl superstition, you will long remember that time while forgetting all the times you saw or heard an owl and nothing of note followed. Once we believe something, our tendency for confirmation bias leads us to notice and remember everything that confirms it while typically ignoring anything that contradicts it.

One highly common belief worldwide, the belief in the Evil Eye, seems especially destructive.[13] This is the belief that when something favorable occurs to someone, another person who is envious may send harmful events their way by wishing them misfortune. Thus, any time a negative event occurs, a search is triggered for the person who caused the misfortune by casting an Evil Eye on the victim, that is, by looking at them with malevolent intent. A wide range of creative and quite beautiful amulets have been created which are believed to help protect the wearer from the Evil Eye (Figure 3.2).

You could argue that belief in the Evil Eye has the practical, useful function of discouraging people from arrogantly flaunting their good fortune lest they inspire envy and resentment in others. Nevertheless, the negative effects of this belief seem likely to be greater. The result of the belief in the Evil Eye is to create a continuous, endless cycle of suspicion, resentment, and vengeance, all rooted in the false belief that you can cause bad things to happen to someone by wishing them ill.

Like superstitions, taboos are beliefs that occur in the imaginary realities of all cultures and provoke anxiety in the believers. There is a vast range of taboos across cultures worldwide.[14] For example, almost all cultures have linguistic taboos, words that must not be spoken or they may cause bad things to happen. Linguistic taboos especially surround words related to the emotionally and socially charged topics of sex and death. Many cultures also have complex taboos regarding menstrual blood, which is believed to have the power to endanger the growth and life of crops, the health of livestock, the success of hunters, and the health and well-being of other people, particularly the menstruating woman's husband. For this reason, menstruating women in many cultures have historically been isolated and forced to remove

Figure 3.2 A child in a village in India wears an amulet to protect against the Evil Eye.

themselves from the presence of others. Food taboos are also common across cultures. There are certain plants and animals that must not be eaten or . . . bad things will result. These beliefs seldom have any basis in fact.

Although they are usually based on false beliefs, it may be that taboos serve a useful function in giving people a sense of control over a potentially chaotic and threatening environment. Even if that control is illusory, the *sense* of control is psychologically beneficial. When people believe they have no control over perilous events and bad things may happen to them no matter what they do, they tend to slide into depression and lassitude; they give up. So taboos may have psychological value even if they are based on misunderstandings of how the physical world works. Nevertheless, the example of menstrual taboos shows that taboos may provoke unfounded anxieties to no useful purpose.

Media-Driven Anxiety: It's a Mean, Mean, Mean, Mean World

Do you remember when the Twin Towers collapsed following the terrorist attacks on September 11, 2001? I still remember it vividly; I expect I always will. I was at the neighborhood playground with our twins, who were about 10 months old at the time, when one of the moms announced that the Towers had been struck. I had no idea what she was talking about it. "Go home and turn on your TV, you'll see," she said. So I did, just in time to watch the second Tower collapse astonishingly into rubble in the space of a few seconds. I remember, too, the stories afterward, for example, of the young man who made it out but went back in to save others and perished along with them. It is still painful to think about now, nearly 25 years later.

About 3,000 people died in the attacks on 9/11. That same year, 2001, over 42,000 Americans died in automobile accidents, and 16,000 were killed in homicides. Nearly all of us saw the Twin Towers collapse, over and over again, on our TVs, whereas our daily homicides are mentioned only in passing on the nightly news, in between the weather and the sports, and auto fatalities are so common that they rarely merit mentioning at all. But terrorist attacks and other mass murders receive such enormous media attention that we fear them far more than we fear more statistically likely threats.

This is the age we live in, an age when a proliferation of stories is presented to us via the media, many of which evoke our anxieties.[15] Since humanity began we have had many immediate sources of anxiety, in threats from the natural environment, animal predators, and other people. We have also long had the images from our imaginary realities as sources of anxiety, in cultural stories told to teach guidelines for behavior and maintain social order. But 500 years ago, with the invention of the printing press, our access to stories began to grow. It grew further as more and more people became literate over the past two centuries, and it took a quantum leap with the transition to electronic media, beginning with the invention of radio about a century ago. Today the internet is a virtually infinite platform for stories, and worldwide we produce them and consume them all day long. On YouTube alone, it would take over 40 *years* for one person to watch all the new content that is posted there *each day*.

There are all kinds of stories in the vast internet world, and many of them trigger our anxieties. They are often intended to do so, in order to catch our attention. "If it bleeds, it leads," as the old journalism adage goes, meaning that it is important to highlight what is most shocking and violent in each day's news in order to capture the attention of potential readers. In recent years, when the COVID-19 pandemic combined with a great deal of political strife and upheaval, "doomscrolling" became a popular new term, meaning scrolling through the day's dire headlines on your phone and finding abundant sources of anxiety and stress.

Researchers on memory have coined two terms to conceptualize our attraction to certain kinds of information over other kinds: *survival information bias* and *social information bias.*[16] Survival information bias is the result of our brains evolving to pay special attention to information that would affect our survival, such as food sources, the most recent location of predators, and territorial boundaries. Early humans who remembered this sort of information best were the most likely to survive and leave progeny that eventually became us. Social information bias derives from the importance of social information in our daily lives. Social information tells us who can be trusted and who cannot, who is most and least capable, who has the highest and lowest status, and so on. According to some theorists, the most recent, most distinctly human parts to develop in our prefrontal cortex were selected for their capacity to identify and process social information, because social information was (and is) of utmost importance for human functioning.

Social information bias and survival information bias are connected: a propensity for noticing and remembering social information would have been important in our species' history for gaining the resources that would promote survival and reproduction. A substantial body of research shows that we remember survival information and social information better than we retain other kinds of information. There is a negativity bias here as well: we are most likely to remember (and share with others) survival and social information that is dire and threatening. People who are high in overall anxiety are especially likely to notice, remember, and share negative information about people and events.

Survival information bias and social information bias clearly served useful functions in guiding our daily lives in the course of our species' evolution. However, in a media-intensive environment, they become radically distorted and provoke fruitless and futile anxieties that assault us daily but provide little benefit. Prior to the modern media era, when our survival information bias or social information bias detected something alarming, we could act on it and protect ourselves because the source of the anxiety was something in our immediate environment. For nearly all our species' history we lived in small groups of a few dozen to a hundred or so people. If something harmful happened to any one of those people, you would definitely want to know about it and remember it, because there was a good chance that it would be a threat to you as well.

Now, however, through electronic media we learn every day about harm and threats that are happening to others worldwide, among all 8 billion of us. But our cognitive judgments, our biases for survival information and social information, are still just like they always were: built to assume that a threat to anyone we "know" must be a potential threat to us as well. Even when we are learning through electronic media about harm to people far away whom we do not know and will never meet, our brain responds with empathy and often with anxiety because we are built to respond *as if* they are part of our circle of a few dozen known others. Consequently, if we pay any attention at all to the news—and nearly all of us do, it is virtually inescapable—we are constantly provoked to anxiety on others' behalf. The natural disaster, the military attack, the political protest that was violently suppressed, the brutal murder, the celebrity who fell victim to drugs or divorce or a spectacular scandal—none of these has any direct relevance to our well-being in our immediate environment, but all of them can *feel* like they do.

In combination, the daily barrage of media content about catastrophes and violence and suffering often makes us feel like the world is a much more threatening and unhappy place than it actually is. Media researcher George

Gerbner memorably conceptualized this as "Mean World Syndrome."[17] Gerbner's theory was first developed in the 1970s and focused on the effects of television violence, but the idea applies equally well to other media, including the internet. Gerbner and others have shown that the more people watch TV, the more likely they are to believe that the world is a dangerous place, that crime rates are high and rising, and that they themselves are at risk of being the victim of a crime. According to Gerbner's theory, they believe this because television often depicts crime and violence on dramas and news shows, which leads viewers to cultivate a view of the world as hostile and dangerous. People's fears of the mean world depicted in the media have no relation to their actual vulnerability to crime and violence. Since 1990 violent crime rates in the United States have plummeted by more than half, but people's fears of being the victim of a violent crime have stayed high.[18] A wise person might want to consider the advice in the John Prine song, to "blow up the TV," or at least occasionally take a break from constant media consumption.

Imagining Menaces: The Twisted Appeal of Conspiracy Theories

A new vaccine had been announced, and in the public response there was much acclaim and relief but also much anxiety and alarm. There were rumors that the vaccine caused the disease rather than preventing it. Some people asserted that the promotion of the vaccine was driven by the greed of the vaccine manufacturers, along with the complicity of the doctors and government officials they were bribing. Opponents of the vaccine started an organization to coordinate their resistance to being legally required to obtain the vaccine for themselves or their children. Many of them declared that the vaccine requirement was a tyrannical infringement on their individual liberty.

Guess the vaccine, the disease, and the era. Zealots worldwide opposing the COVID-19 vaccine in 2021–2022? Affluent liberal California parents resisting the school requirement to vaccinate their children for measles in the 1990s? Americans doubting the value of the polio vaccine in the mid-20th century? The British questioning the smallpox vaccine in the mid-19th century?

The answer is all of the above.[19] From a scientific perspective, the discovery of vaccines is indisputably the greatest medical advance ever. In a short time, vaccines have virtually eliminated numerous diseases that had killed people, especially children, with horrible effectiveness and in enormous numbers for centuries. Yet vaccines have frequently been the subject of widely held conspiracy theories. To many people in every era, vaccines are not the greatest medical invention of all time but an evil and insidious threat to humanity (Figure 3.3).

The anti-vax conspiracy theory is not the only popular conspiracy theory of our time, and it is not even close to being the looniest.[20] Here are some others that have been popular in the past century:

- A UFO from another part of the universe crashed in Roswell, New Mexico, and the vehicle and its non-earthly inhabitants were quickly whisked away by the U.S. Air Force.
- President John F. Kennedy was assassinated not by a deluded loner but as part of a complex secret plot involving the CIA, Fidel Castro, the Mafia, and Vice President Lyndon Johnson.

Figure 3.3 Since the first vaccines were invented, there have been conspiracy theories claiming they do more harm than good.

- American astronauts did not really land on the moon in 1969. The so-called moon landing actually took place on a movie set in Hollywood.
- The federal government is secretly run by a cabal of liberal elites who use their power to promote cannibalism, Satanism, and pedophilia.

To anyone who does not believe them, conspiracy theories are obviously ludicrous. So why do so many people believe such things? There are plenty of legitimate sources of anxiety, in our time and any other, so why would we want to create additional frightful phantoms that do not exist?

Beliefs in conspiracy theories can be understood as another overheated version of the useful motivation we all have to construct an imaginary reality that makes sense of a complex and confusing world. The world around us is chaotic and overwhelming in its raw state, so we look for patterns, and we look for the sources of those patterns. We construct a story that will allow us to believe we understand the world and can at least partially control it. That belief is extremely important to our psychological stability and well-being.

We are constantly looking for and creating explanations for why the world functions as it does, why things that happen around us are happening, the root causes, the underlying forces. Evolutionary psychologists call this cognitive tendency *agency detection*. We are always trying to detect the agents who are causing events to happen. In our original evolutionary environment that meant trying to determine why the spring ran dry or why the nuts or tubers we relied on in our diet were abundant one year but scarce the next. Sometimes our pursuit of agency detection leads us to quasi-scientific explanations—the nuts failed to grow because there was too little or too much rain here, so let's look somewhere else—and sometimes it leads us to invent an explanation: we failed to make the proper sacrifices to our ancestors, so they thwarted the growth of our tubers in a fit of pique.

Supernatural explanations are a consequence of *hyperactive agency detection*, our cognitive tendency to invent an explanation if no good explanation is apparent in what we can observe or deduce directly.[21] So are conspiracy theories. Above all, we hate to admit "I don't know. I have no idea why these things happened. It's all beyond my comprehension." Especially in our modern, complex world, where we are inundated daily with information through multiple media sources, we are strongly motivated to come up with some kind of overarching explanation that will allow us to make sense of it all. Conspiracy theories provide this kind of explanation.

Once we latch on to a conspiracy theory, confirmation bias leads us to notice information that reinforces it and ignore or dismiss information that contradicts it. This confirmation bias is especially prominent in the internet era. When the only news available was from three television stations and one or two local daily newspapers, it was hard to avoid colliding daily with information that provided a reality check on whatever unhinged conspiracy theory might have been brewing in your brain. Conspiracy theories still blossomed sometimes among some people, but in the internet era it is easier than ever for people to find their way to bizarre ideas and then enter an information loop where they are offered more and more that confirms the theory and they can completely ignore any naysayers.

Not everyone is equally susceptible to conspiracy theories, of course. Research has shown that people are more likely to believe in conspiracy theories if they are male, unmarried, have low educational attainment, have low income, are unemployed, and have weak social networks.[22] People are also more likely to believe in conspiracy theories if they are part of a group that they perceive as being undervalued, disrespected, and under threat. And sometimes the powers-that-be really are out to get you: it is not irrational for people in low-status groups to believe that the people in the dominant groups are contemptuous of them and are seeking to deceive and exploit them, even if the specific form the conspiracy theory takes is not rooted in reality.

The relation between anxiety and conspiracy theories is complex. Conspiracy theories arouse anxiety by asserting threats that do not actually exist. That's obvious enough. To return to the vaccine example, millions of parents worldwide have been spurred to anxiety over the past century as a consequence of false claims about the supposed dangers of vaccines to their children. But conspiracy theories also assuage anxiety by giving the believer a way of making sense of a complex and confusing world.

I am not saying conspiracy theories are good after all. They do a lot of damage by provoking unfounded anger and hostility and by leading people to make fantasy-based decisions that are destructive to themselves and others.[23] What I am saying is that part of their appeal is that they give people assurance that the world is comprehensible. Conspiracy theories make people feel that the world may be full of threats, but at least they are aware of those threats and can understand them and prepare for them. Like imaginary realities more generally, conspiracy theories distort reality but provide psychological consolation.

It is also important to acknowledge that the basic premise of conspiracy theories, which is that authorities are not telling the whole story and that important information is being concealed from public view, is sometimes valid. The U.S. government really did enroll hundreds of Black men with syphilis in a study in the 1930s and never told them, for a period of *40 years*, that they were receiving only placebos in order for "scientists" to see what happened to people whose syphilis went untreated. The Soviet Union really did create a "gulag archipelago" in the 1960s and 1970s where thousands of political prisoners were held in isolation. The Catholic Church really did cover up for decades an appalling, vast scandal of child sexual molestation throughout the priesthood, worldwide (and still has not come clean about it). Numerous other examples are available from governments, religious institutions, and other powerful organizations. The fact that suspicions that elites are up to no good are *sometimes* valid is psychological fuel enough for conspiracy theorists to propose many far-fetched claims that have no validity whatsoever but nevertheless attract many adherents.

Fear Can Be Fun: Anxiety as a Stimulant

What is the scariest movie you have ever seen? For me it is *Wait Until Dark*, which I saw when I was 12 years old at some kind of middle school recreation event. It stars Audrey Hepburn as a blind woman being stalked by a killer for reasons I don't remember. At the end the killer finds her, but she manages to cut the lights, giving her the advantage. My friends and I screamed and laughed and grabbed each other in delighted terror, especially in that final scene. (Spoiler alert: Audrey won.)

Why did we willingly spend two hours watching a movie that scared the pants off us? Because it was fun. That's the obvious answer. What's less obvious is the answer to the question "*Why* was it fun?" Don't we normally avoid putting ourselves into situations where we are scared out of our wits and our anxiety is off the charts?

The relation between anxiety and enjoyment is complex and variable. Clearly, we sometimes enjoy the stimulation of high anxiety. If we did not, we would not willingly place ourselves in imaginary situations designed to provoke anxiety, fear, and horror and call it "entertainment." We have been doing this for thousands of years. The oldest known form of drama is tragedy. Twenty-five hundred years ago people gathered willingly—even eagerly—to watch Oedipus unwittingly commit the horrifying violation of having sexual relations with his mother, then stab his own eyes out when he realized what he had done. Shakespeare's most renowned plays are the tragedies, not the comedies, and at the end of every tragedy people die violently, including many characters you had grown rather fond of. Novels nearly always involve provocative, shocking events outside the realm of our normal experience; "happily ever after" is the end of a story, never the beginning, because there is nothing anxiety-provoking about people living happily, and therefore nothing interesting or engaging. Today the lists of the most popular films each year include many that portray people in terrifying situations, and the killing and dying that happens to them in those situations (Figure 3.4).

We enjoy having our anxiety stimulated by shocking entertainment because when it is in the context of entertainment the anxiety is manageable and controlled.[24] We willingly enter the imaginary reality offered by the performance, but we know all along it is fictional. Much as we may be fascinated by watching Oedipus stumble around blind on stage, we know the actor playing Oedipus is not really blind and will appear for the curtain call at the end of the play, fully recovered. We engage deeply with characters in films

Figure 3.4 People often seek out anxiety-provoking imaginary realities in entertainment.

as they experience excruciating things, and we feel cognitively, emotionally, and physically aroused, even though we know full well that in the end it is "just a movie." Yet while the show is occurring we immerse ourselves in it, empathizing with the characters and through our empathy gaining some sense of what it would be like to experience those extreme situations and the extreme emotions that result. This allows us to pleasurably expand the range of our imaginary experiences beyond the mostly tame experiences that constitute our daily lives.

Heaven Would Be Hell: Why We Need Anxiety for a Full Life

In the major world religions, depictions of the afterlife are diverse, but they have one thing in common: no anxieties. For Jews, it entails wandering around in Sheol, the underworld, which is gloomy and dreary but at least there is nothing to be anxious about. For Christians, there is constant singing of praise at the foot of the throne of God, which sounds like it would be thrilling . . . for about five minutes. In Islam, the afterlife is a lush paradise where cool streams run and food and drink are abundant, sort of like being on a perpetual cruise down the Nile. In Hinduism and Buddhism, we are reincarnated back to earth until we achieve the spiritual enlightenment that allows us to step off this treadmill and dissolve into the One, obliterating our individual identity. It may not be much fun, but at least that is the end of anxiety.

To those of us currently bound to the earth, with all its daily anxieties, stresses, pains, and disappointments, an afterlife free of all such strife may sound awfully good. The prospect of eventual peace and serenity is an appealing part of the imaginary realities offered in nearly all cultures. But would we really think so, in actuality? Everyone likes the idea of a few days of lounging and relaxation, but few people aspire to stretch that to months or years, much less to eternity. Even people who are retired are happiest when they find self-directed ways to challenge themselves and engage with the world. Our true psychological ideal is not zero anxiety but the sweet spot of anxiety, where we are engaged and motivated, using our capacities to their limit but not overwhelmed.

One way this has been framed in psychology is with the concept of *sensation seeking.*[25] This is a personality trait defined by the extent of a person's appetite for *novelty* and *intensity* of sensation. Novelty includes experiences such as traveling to unusual places, trying unfamiliar foods, and meeting people from outside your usual circle. Intensity includes experiences such as listening to loud, raucous music, taking an amusement park ride that entails high speed and lots of abrupt twists and turns, and gambling for high stakes. People vary in sensation seeking, so that an experience that provokes unpleasant anxiety for one person may be the height of enjoyment for another.

The reason that heaven would be hell is that we are not just anxiety-prone; we are anxiety-*seeking*. Our brain, and our hormonal and physiological systems, did not evolve so that no stimulation is our ideal; they evolved to seek out informationally useful stimulation, to engage with the world and use our abilities to address the challenges before us, and anxiety is one of our key motivators for that engagement. No anxiety would mean no goals, no challenges, no satisfaction in the summoning and mobilizing of our abilities.

In sum, the bad news is that we will never create a paradise here on earth. Our imagination will always invent possible threats, even when no actual threats are present, and those threats will always inspire anxiety. The good news is that most of us would not want to live in paradise even if we could. Our imaginary realities console us with the prospect of perpetual bliss, but the consolation works only because perpetual bliss never arrives. A few days after entering heaven we would be applying to be transferred back to our stressful, anxiety-provoking, complicated, exasperating, exciting earth.

4
Moral Egoism
Imagining Ourselves on the Side of the Angels

- He may have been convicted of the biggest swindle in history, but Bernie Madoff apparently does not feel bad about what he did. "Fuck my victims," he is reported to have told a fellow inmate.[1] All he had done, he explained, was take money from people who were rich and greedy and wanted even more. In other words, he gave them what they deserved. It may seem wrong and bad to some, but it was actually right and good.
- Many American presidents have done things that could be considered morally questionable, but Richard Nixon is the only one forced to resign for obstruction of justice and other violations of his oath of office. Nevertheless, he did not see himself as the bad guy in that scenario. On the contrary, he explained in a 1977 interview. If he was guilty of anything, it was of being too soft-hearted toward his co-conspirators and their families: "Maybe I defended them too long, maybe I tried to help them too much, but I was concerned about them, I was concerned about their families." The real bad guys were his vicious and ruthless enemies: "I gave them a sword, and they stuck it in and they twisted it with relish."[2]
- Imelda Marcos, first lady of the Philippines from 1965 to 1986, is perhaps best known for owning 3.000 pairs of shoes, but she disputed this, claiming to have had merely 1,060 at her peak (Figure 4.1). She and her husband, President Ferdinand Marcos, were accused of looting the Filipino treasury of $10 billion during their time in power. She denied this as well, confidently stating that "when you are at peace with the truth and you know that you are on the side of the right and God is on your side, you are not afraid of anything, including jail." And even if she had bent the rules a bit, she had good reasons. "Doesn't the fight for survival also justify swindle and theft? In self-defense, anything goes." She believed her enjoyment of an abundant material life

Imaginary Realities. Jeffrey Jensen Arnett, Oxford University Press. © Jeffrey Jensen Arnett (2026).
DOI: 10.1093/9780197817407.003.0004

Figure 4.1 According to Imelda Marcos, her ostentatious lifestyle was morally justified.

> required no apologies. "I was born ostentatious. They will list my name in the dictionary someday. They will use Imeldific to mean ostentatious extravagance."[3]

Not all of our constructions of imaginary realities involve supernatural beings or magical forces. In fact, some of our most serious and dangerous distortions of reality are in our self-perceptions and our social relations, above all in the arena of morality. We are used to thinking of morality as one of the features that make us humans venerable and raise us above the mere beasts. To be "moral" means to be "good." But in this chapter I will show that we have a propensity for *moral egoism* that is perhaps our most dangerous quality. It allows us to excuse almost anything we do and gives us license to do harm to others, both as individuals and as groups. We not only excuse harmful acts; we feel good about them, confident that we are on the side of the angels. It can be darkly amusing to hear others defend themselves in ways that obviously smack of self-serving biases, but those biases are never so obvious when they are our own. Bernie. Nixon. Imelda. Me. You.

Although moral egoism is a new concept, there is a great deal of theorizing and research in psychology that provides evidence for it. This includes the well-established areas of cognitive dissonance, social comparisons, and social identity, as well as recent studies on how individuals and groups make sense of—and justify—their own moral thoughts and actions. Together, these areas provide abundant evidence of moral egoism as a fundamental feature of our imaginary realities. The contribution of the concept of moral egoism is to tie together the theory and research in all these areas in an original form that highlights their *moral* implications.

Importantly, moral egoism fuses individual and group moral thinking as none of the other theories do. At the group level, moral egoism is the belief that our group is right and good, and groups that oppose us are wrong and bad. Just as individual moral egoism is a potent source of interpersonal conflict, so group moral egoism is evident in human history and even today in group conflict and collective violence, including war and genocide. Yet, like other aspects of our imaginary realities, both individual and group moral egoism are more than just a strange and twisted defect of human psychology. Both forms of moral egoism confer an advantage in competition with others. Believing we are on the side of all that is good and right provides a motivational advantage and allows us to pursue our interests with unfettered zeal. First let's examine individual moral egoism, then the link from individual to group moral egoism, then the features of group moral egoism.

The Moral Egoism of Individuals

At the individual level, moral egoism means that people have a strong tendency to view their beliefs, attitudes, and actions as morally right and good. Let's start our examination of individual moral egoism by looking at how theories and research on cognitive dissonance and social comparisons can help us understand it.

Moral Egoism and Cognitive Dissonance

When was the last time you had a serious conflict with someone? Reflecting on that conflict now, who do you think was right and who was wrong? When was the last time you told someone "I'm sorry" or "I was wrong"? Was this difficult or easy for you to say?

Answering these kinds of questions will give you a good idea of what I mean by moral egoism. If you are like most people, your assessment of most of your conflicts will conclude with the judgment that you were right and the other person was wrong. You also likely find it difficult to say "I was wrong" or "I'm sorry." Some people *never* do. Why do we have this tendency to skew our moral judgments in our favor? Isn't it obviously destructive to our relations with others? Why do we have such trouble admitting we are wrong, when doing so could help smooth over conflicts and restore harmonious relations?

Toward answering these questions we can make use of Leon Festinger's theory of *cognitive dissonance*. As stated in previous chapters, the concept of cognitive dissonance proposes that holding two incompatible views makes us uneasy, and we seek to resolve this conflict by changing one of them, even if that means distorting reality.[4] Festinger emphasized the cognitive basis of this dissonance, seeing it as a problem of resolving two inconsistent views of an event or problem, but theorists and researchers after him have emphasized the more personal, emotional, and social aspects of it. In Elliot Aronson's influential reworking of Festinger's theory, the real dissonance is between the person's self-concept and their behavior: "I am a good person, yet it appears that I have done something wrong."[5] Aronson's theory assumes that most people have a positive self-concept, so they experience dissonance when they behave in ways that could be seen—by themselves and others—as incompetent or immoral. This inconsistency typically provokes *self-justifications*, the explanations we invent as we squirm to avoid taking personal responsibility for actions that could be viewed as mistaken, harmful, or wrong. Aronson's self-consistency theory is related to the idea of moral egoism, but moral egoism stresses that the source of the discomfort is essentially moral, not merely a problem of self-consistency.

One common arena that vividly displays people's self-justifying moral egoism is their accounts of divorce. Marriage is at the heart of most adults' emotional and social lives and a key part of their identity, so marriages rarely sink without a few explosions along the way. Ask divorced couples what happened, and you often find them to be on different planets. He worked all the time, she says. All she cared about was money, so I had to work two jobs, he says. We split up because she had an affair, he says. Nonsense, says she; he wanted to drink and hang out with his buddies all the time, so eventually I gave up and found someone else. In one study of couples' reasons for their divorce, people were over six times more likely to blame their partner than to blame themselves.[6] In another study, divorced people typically framed themselves as "victim" and their ex as the "villain" in their split.[7]

The self-justifying response to divorce can be a way of protecting one's mental health. As with other aspects of imaginary realities, the distortions of facts involved in moral egoism may be inaccurate, but they can nevertheless be constructive and useful. Blaming yourself may be more honest in some cases, but heaped on top of the searing pain of ending a marriage, it can cause people to slide down further into suffering and despair. Generally, people function better following divorce if they believe the other person, not themselves, was most to blame.[8] Even if that is not an accurate account of what happened, this kind of individual moral egoism can help people restore a sense of control and self-respect that enables them to move forward and recover.

Moral Egoism and Social Comparisons

Another important source of insights on individual moral egoism can be found in research on *social comparisons*, which involve people's tendency to compare themselves favorably to others. Research has shown that people tend to evaluate themselves positively in comparison to "other people," the so-called Better Than Average Effect, rating themselves as more intelligent, more competent, more friendly, and so on.[9] They also apply this tendency in the moral arena, generally viewing themselves as being morally better than other people. For example, one study asked American adults about the likelihood that they or "others" would engage in behaviors that are "immoral" (e.g., lying to a coworker).[10] They found that people generally viewed themselves as less likely than others to commit the immoral acts.

People also show this tendency to elevate themselves morally when they reflect on their own moral experiences. One study focused on expressions of anger and asked American undergraduates to recount a "victim" story and a "perpetrator" story based on their own experiences of angering someone or being angered by someone.[11] Participants almost always believed that their anger as "perpetrator" was justified and rarely conceded that it was immoral or deliberately hurtful. When they did admit error they sought to excuse or minimize it. In contrast, in their "victim" stories almost none of them viewed the perpetrator's anger toward them as justified. Although it was framed as a study of anger, not morality, this is a clear demonstration of moral egoism, reflecting the tendency to view conflicts from a self-interested and self-justifying perspective.

Another study asked American adults about the "worst thing" and the "most unkind thing" they had ever done, as well as the worst and most unkind things ever done to them.[12] Participants generally viewed what had been done to them as worse than what they had done. Moral egoism was also evident in their explanations for the behaviors. Specifically, in comparison to the person who had done wrong to them, they viewed themselves as less likely to repeat the bad behavior, and also viewed their behaviors as less reflective of who they "really are" as a person. This finding matches other recent studies showing that people generally believe they have a "true self" that is morally good and that occasional misbehaviors or immoral acts are aberrations that do not reflect or diminish the good true self.[13]

Social comparisons favoring ourselves are such a sturdy part of our imaginary realities that they can even be found among criminals. You might think that it would be hard to sustain moral egoism's twisted self-perception when you have not only done bad things but have been tried, convicted, and imprisoned for them, but it actually turns out to be easy. One study found that prisoners convicted mostly of serious crimes such as assault or robbery rated themselves favorably on a variety of moral traits, such as trustworthiness, kindness, and compassion, not just compared to the average prisoner but compared to the average community member—although they did concede that they were only "average" on "law-abidingness."[14] Other research has founded similar tendencies among "white-collar" criminals, guilty of offenses such as fraud and embezzlement, who frame their illegal acts not as wrong but as necessary to prevail in fierce competition with others.[15]

Strategies of Individual Moral Egoism

In addition to research on criminals that uses the social comparisons framework, there is a large body of research on criminals' views of their morality that provides abundant evidence for moral egoism. Criminologists use the term *neutralization* for the ways people involved in criminal activities attempt to find moral justifications for what they have done.[16] The concept was originally developed in studies of young criminals in the 1950s, and later expanded to apply to white-collar criminals as well. A lot of what these studies describe as neutralization is similar to what I mean here by moral egoism, as it involves people skewing their moral assessments in their own favor. But "neutralization" is a poor word for it. People do not just "neutralize" the moral threat that comes from the realization that they have behaved immorally; they find ways to twist the moral calculation so that they believe what they did was justified.

Studies of criminals' perceptions of their morality confirm their moral egoism, but the interpretations of these studies often mistakenly assume that their excuses for wrong behavior are exclusive to criminals. Here are some of the specific strategies of "neutralization" identified by researchers, along with a few others I have added.[17] See if they sound familiar from your experiences with other people's moral egoism—and your own.

Denial of Responsibility. It wasn't my intention to harm anyone. I was under a lot of stress. I was going through a difficult time. I didn't do anything bad, I just happened to be among people who were doing something bad, so I got blamed, too.

Denial of Harm. Nobody really got hurt. You make it sound a lot worse than it actually was.

Condemning the Condemners. Wait, *you're* accusing *me*? What you did was a lot worse. You don't have any right to be accusing me of doing something wrong, after all you've done.

Just Deserts. I only gave them what they deserved. They needed to pay for what they did.

It Could Have Been Worse. I could have done a lot more than I did, but I chose not to. Don't I deserve some credit for that? Look at all the times I could have done it again, but I didn't.

Not My True Self. That wasn't the real me. That wasn't like me at all. I don't know what got into me.

Redirection. You make it seem like I'm a horrible person, but what about all the good things I've done? Everybody makes mistakes. You're pointing to one mistake over and over, but outside of that I've been a good parent/son/daughter/partner/coworker/neighbor/friend.

Appeal to Higher Loyalties. I didn't do it for my sake; I did it to protect my child/partner/friend/coworkers/other loved ones. It was my duty. I had a job to do, so I did it the best I could. If I hadn't done it, innocent people would have been harmed.

Dehumanization. My victims aren't even human. They are more like vermin, insects, or other dangerous pests. They're like a disease that needs to be eradicated. So what I did to them was actually good, not bad.

Does this list of expressions of individual moral egoism sound uncomfortably familiar? It's not just criminals who try to wash themselves clean of any feeling of wrongdoing; it's all of us. It is part of the psychological human condition. But with rare exceptions, we are not psychopaths who *never* admit to being wrong. Moral egoism is part of the distortions of our imaginary realities, but like our other imaginary realities there are limits to it.

The Limits of Moral Egoism

Not everyone exhibits moral egoism all the time or to the same degree. Our fundamental psychological qualities are widespread tendencies, not traits that are universal, uniform, and unalterable. In the case of moral egoism, people vary in the degree to which they have this tendency. We all know people who never admit they were wrong, ever, as well as people who seem quick to admit they were wrong—even when they really were not—and say "I'm sorry" readily, even when they really should not.

Even among criminals, over half admit to feeling at least some guilt for the behavior that resulted in their conviction.[18] Most of the rest of us can certainly remember things we did that we now regret and regard as wrong. In studies that ask people to recall the "worst thing" they have ever done, no one has any trouble coming up with something. In short, people can feel guilt and regret over some of the things they have done, even as they also defend and excuse many other things they have done that might be regarded by others as wrong.

Admitting we were wrong can help resolve conflict and can feel psychologically cleansing. So why don't people acknowledge their moral errors more often and more easily? Why does moral egoism get in the way? Because admitting you were wrong also means a loss of power. It is a form of social submission. And although it may feel psychologically cleansing and allow you to move on, guilt, remorse, and regret are unpleasant feelings. It feels better to say, if only to yourself, "No, *dammit*, I was right and they were wrong!" Resolving your moral dissonance by deciding that you were in the right makes you feel invigorated and motivated to excel and outmaneuver your adversaries. That is why it is part of the psychology of human nature. Like other aspects of imaginary realities, moral egoism was selected for in the course of human evolution because it confers an advantage in competition with others.

The Development of Individual Moral Egoism

My wife Lene and I bought a nice leather chair for our living room when our twins, Paris and Miles, turned four years old, thinking that by now they were old enough to know they should be gentle with a nice piece of furniture. Wrong! Within two weeks they had put several large scratches in it. When confronted, they confessed at first, but then retracted their confession and looked for an alibi. "We didn't do it, Daddy," claimed Paris, lawyer for the defense. "Well, then who did?" I demanded. She cast her eyes down, as if it were painful for her to reveal the true offender. "Santa Claus," she confessed.

Paris was by no means unusual in exercising individual moral egoism at a young age. By age three, most children recount their conflicts with siblings in ways that portray them as in the right and their siblings as wrong. More generally, from early childhood onward children seek to excuse and defend their violations of rules and norms, often by blaming others.

Theory and research on moral socialization show how children learn the moral standards of their culture. At the heart of this process across cultures is learning to behave in prosocial ways and restrain self-interest. This includes learning to experience "healthy guilt" when violating moral norms and behaving selfishly.[19] Healthy guilt acts as a deterrent to selfish behavior, and the desire to avoid guilt provides an incentive for being kind and considerate to others. Feelings and verbal expressions of guilt appear in early childhood. However, guilt is aversive, so there is also a motivation to evade it from an early age. It can be evaded by following social norms and avoiding selfish behavior, but also by exercising moral egoism, that is, by framing moral events in a self-justifying way.

With age, children increasingly learn and adhere to the social norms of their culture, but they also get better at exercising individual moral egoism to avoid blame and guilt. As children grow in their social and cognitive abilities, their strategies of moral egoism become similarly more complex as they seek to deflect not only external punishments but internal guilt. For example, in a study of Swiss children ages five and nine, the older children were more likely than the younger ones to justify their own transgressions, most often claiming they were merely retaliating for wrongs done to them.[20] Already from a young age we are adept at individual moral egoism, and it is a psychological skill we get better at with age. We stop blaming things on Santa Claus and find more subtle and effective ways to deflect and deny blame and guilt.

Moral Egoism Across Cultures and History

As we have seen, studies inspired by cognitive dissonance theory and social comparisons theory provide abundant material for understanding the features of individual moral egoism. These studies show that the human tendency toward moral egoism is already well-established under other names that have insufficiently recognized their moral dimensions.

Unfortunately, like most psychological research, nearly all of the studies in these areas have been conducted on an extremely narrow range of the human population, mainly today's American adults—especially undergraduates in American research universities—which is hardly an adequate basis for a theory intended to apply broadly to humanity.[21] There is a need, then, to place individual moral egoism in a broader cultural and historical framework in order to examine whether it is a widespread human tendency and to see the forms it may take across times and places. Doing so will also enable us to establish the connections between individual and group moral egoism.

Both cognitive dissonance theory and social comparisons theory assume that most people have a positive self-concept that needs defending against signs that the person has done anything that could be construed as bad or wrong. Moral egoism helps protect the individual in the comfortable belief that the "true self" is good and right, despite any evidence to the contrary. However, research supporting the assumption of a positive self-concept has also been conducted mainly on Americans, the usual suspects. If a positive self-concept is not a human universal but an artifact of living in the United States and other Western societies today, then it could be that cognitive dissonance theory, social comparisons theory, and individual moral egoism likewise apply only to an unusual minority of the human population.

Historians and sociologists provide an unambiguous answer to our question. Yes, the positive self-concept is a modern invention, founded in the *individualism* that sprang out of the Enlightenment beginning in Europe about 300 years ago.[22] One of the ideas that came out of the Enlightenment was the radical notion that individuals have value in their own right, irrespective of their membership in groups like family, community, and religion. By now, individualism is common enough that it shows up routinely in the form of the positive self-concepts of Americans participating in psychological studies.

However, throughout the long run of human history it is clear that a childhood environment *discouraging* a positive self-concept has been part of the human experience nearly always and everywhere, and still is in most places. All the major religions teach that we are born with morally errant tendencies and are in need of moral correction and instruction. Within families, the process of *socialization*—teaching children how to be a member of a culture—always entails, at least in part, telling children to stop doing what they are tempted to do and adhere instead to the rules promoted by others. It is through socialization that our imaginary realities are first created—in the beliefs we learn about the world around us (and its supernatural and magical forces) as well as in how we construct our self-perceptions. Through socialization children learn to restrain their tendency to moral egoism and instead adhere to what their parents, grandparents, siblings, and others tell them to do. Through socialization you learn not only to behave as others want but to think as they want, including in your perceptions of yourself. That is, you construct an imaginary reality in which the group is good but you are not, and your duty is to restrain your deplorable self-interest and put the group's interests first.

The dominant form of cultural socialization worldwide has always been and still is toward discouraging self-enhancing tendencies and promoting group interests and the value of *interdependence*, not independence. Studies of the history of childhood show a strong emphasis on socialization based on values of obedience and conformity throughout human history, until very recent times.[23] Even in the United States, long renowned for its individualism, values promoting interdependence were prevalent well into the 20th century. In the famous Middletown studies, conducted in the same Midwestern American town 50 years apart, the top values parents sought to teach their children in 1928 were obedience, loyalty to church, and good manners; by 1978 the top values were independence and tolerance.[24] Since the 1970s the emphasis on individualism and promoting a positive self-concept has grown even more in the United States and other Western countries, as parents and teachers increasingly regard it as their top goal to help children learn to feel good about themselves.

But even in the modern era this goal is unusual among the world's societies, and promoting values of obedience, conformity, and submission is still the main way that adults socialize children. In one famous anthropological study, Beatrice Whiting and Carolyn Pope Edwards and their colleagues observed processes of socialization in 12 communities around the world.[25] One of their most interesting and important findings with implications for moral egoism is that mothers across cultures seldom praised their children—except in the suburban United States, where praise was common. In the other cultures, mothers feared that praising their children would make them "proud"—a vice, in their view, not a virtue. In other words, they consciously avoided socializing their children to have a positive self-concept.

Instead, children were socialized, through example as well as through commands and reprimands, to learn how to mute their own self-interests and cooperate well with others. They learned to feel good about themselves not because of their individual worth and accomplishments but because of how they helped others and did what they were told. This kind of socialization prepared children to take on important responsibilities from an early age. Young children were indulged and nurtured for the first three years of life, but by age four they were assisting their parents or older siblings in daily tasks, and by ages six to ten older children were often primarily responsible for the care of younger siblings, among other duties. By their teens, the traditional pattern in human societies is that both girls and boys are doing near-adult work, girls alongside women and boys alongside men.

You can see, then, how in the traditional way of socializing children, a positive self-concept and the individual moral egoism it may generate would be disruptive to group cooperation and the smooth functioning of family, village, and society. There may indeed be a universal tendency toward a positive self-concept, represented in individual moral egoism, but in most cultures that tendency is tempered or even inverted in the course of childhood socialization.

Connecting Individual and Group Moral Egoism

Is this account of socialization for interdependence inconsistent with the claim of widespread moral egoism? No, it just means that individual moral egoism is usually shaped in the course of early socialization into group moral egoism. In a culture that values interdependence—most of the world today, and all the world until very recently—socialization reshapes children's inborn, natural tendency to believe "I am right and good" and instead teaches them "No, you are wrong and bad, but you are part of us, and *we* are right and good."

But is it really possible to take an inherent tendency to believe "I am right and good" and turn it on its head like that? It's not only possible; it's easy. What makes it easy is that we are born with such a strong readiness to learn from others how to make sense of the world, such an open canvas on which to paint an imaginary reality. We are not like other animals, which are born with all sorts of abilities and reflexive behaviors that are ready for a particular environmental niche and so either do not need to be taught or require very little teaching. Instead, as cultural animals we are born prepared to learn any of a wide range of skills for surviving and adapting on the fly to the environment in which we happen to have been born, whether a mountain or a tropical forest, an arctic tundra or a desert. This includes a readiness to learn how to see ourselves and our place in the world. So when parents, grandparents, siblings, and others in our social world tell us from the beginning, "You were born wrong and bad," we believe.

What makes it possible for us to believe this without simply giving up and withering away in early childhood is that it always comes with the consolation "but you are part of us, and *we* are right and good." This is how the energy and emotion of individual moral egoism becomes translated into the cohesion and conformity of group moral egoism.

The Moral Egoism of Groups

Martin Luther, the Protestant leader of the 16th century, at first sympathized with the Jews for refusing to embrace Christianity (Figure 4.2). After all, in his view, for centuries it had been thoroughly corrupted by Popes and the Church. However, once he and his allies had cleaned it up, they believed there was no longer a moral basis for Jews to continue to reject the Christian faith. When the Jews decided instead to remain Jewish, he unleashed a stream of invective upon them that was hugely influential throughout Europe and continues to reverberate in our time. "What shall we Christians do?" in the face of such obstinacy, he wondered in 1543 in *On the Jews and Their Lies.* Then he offered his "sincere advice": as a first step, "set fire to their synagogues or schools and bury and cover with dirt whatever will not burn,

Figure 4.2 Martin Luther justified his attacks on Jews by saying it would be "wrong to be merciful" to them if they rejected Christianity.

so that no man will ever again see a stone or cinder of them." Such vandalism would be committed for the highest moral reasons, of course. "This is to be done in honor of our Lord and of Christendom, so that God might see that we are Christians, and do not condone or knowingly tolerate such public lying, cursing, and blaspheming." Doing so "would demonstrate to God our serious resolve . . . that we have now given them their due reward." Next, "their houses [would] also be razed and destroyed" and "all cash and treasure of silver and gold be taken from them and put aside for safekeeping."[26]

He further advised "our rulers" to regard the Jews as a kind of disease and "act like a good physician who, when gangrene has set in, proceeds without mercy to cut, saw, and burn flesh, veins, bone, and marrow." This, too, would be right and proper, because "it would be wrong to be merciful and confirm them in their conduct." If even this treatment did not enlighten them, "we must drive them out like mad dogs, so that we do not become partakers of their abominable blasphemy and all their other vices and thus merit God's wrath and be damned with them." Luther had no doubt his exhortations to persecute the Jews were divinely blessed: "I have done my duty. . . . I am exonerated."[27]

Luther's wrathful rants on the Jews of his time are shocking and appalling, but alas not unique or even unusual in human history. Nor are they merely part of the regrettable human past; similar language is used to justify group persecution in our time, as we shall soon see. Although advocating collective violence is group moral egoism in its most extreme form, a wide spectrum of group moral egoism is a standard part of our imaginary realities. Just as there is an individual tendency to believe that "I" am right and those who disagree or oppose me are wrong, so there is a group tendency to believe that "our" ways and beliefs are right and good, and the ways and beliefs of other groups are bad and wrong.

Social Identity and Group Moral Egoism

This tendency for group moral egoism is well-established from several decades of theory and research on *social identity*. According to social identity theory, first articulated by Henri Tajfel in the 1970s, the human cognitive ability for categorization is applied early in life to thinking of oneself as a member of a variety of groups, defined by family, community, ethnicity, religion, nationality, and so on.[28] By age five, children have a well-established social identity based on their group memberships. From childhood onward, people are aware of their social identities and derive emotional value and meaning from them. Social identity enhances the cohesion of groups and makes them more productive.

However, social identity also deepens distinctions, competition, and hostility between groups. According to Tajfel, in developing a social identity people exaggerate both the similarities within their group and the differences between their group and other groups. This leads to social comparisons on the group level, in which people compare their group favorably to other groups, enhancing the positive features of their *ingroup* and the negative features of any competing *outgroup*. Decades of research by Tajfel and many others have shown how readily people of all ages embrace group membership, even based on superficial and temporary distinctions, and subsequently engage in social comparisons.[29] These social comparisons then become the basis of competition, opposition, hatred, and even violent conflict between groups.

The theory of moral egoism proposes that social comparisons based on social identity become especially fierce when they have a moral basis. It may be relatively harmless to view your group's food, language, style of dress, or sports team as "better" than those of neighboring groups, but social comparisons become much more serious and hostile when they frame "us" as morally just and "them" as morally corrupt. Social comparisons that involve moral issues—moral egoism at the group level—have been found in many studies to have strong motivational force and to be accompanied by intense emotions, as the Luther quotes that began this section chillingly display. A social identity that is morally charged arouses an especially strong ingroup-outgroup distinction. People respond to an awareness of these kinds of social comparisons with intolerance, an attempt to increase social and physical distance from the opposing group, and lowered levels of intergroup cooperativeness and goodwill.[30]

Natural, Normal, and Necessary: Justifying Group Moral Egoism

When the first European voyagers to what came to be called North America were busy "discovering" their new continent, they came upon the inconvenient fact that other people were already living there. Today we might call it ethnic cleansing, or even genocide, but to early Americans the removal of indigenous peoples from land they had lived on for generations was a practical necessity, and morally defensible. To George Washington it was as necessary to kill Indians as it would be to kill any dangerous animal, because "Indians and wolves are both beasts of prey, tho' they differ in shape."[31] Thomas Jefferson concurred, warning ominously, "If ever we are constrained to lift the hatchet against any tribe, we will never lay it down till that tribe is exterminated. . . . [T]hey will kill some of us; we shall destroy them all."[32]

Most notoriously, President Andrew Jackson led the ethnic cleansing of Native Americans from the southern states during the 1830s, a project he pursued with self-righteous zeal (Figure 4.3). In his eyes this was not a brutal, cruel, racist exercise of raw power, but an opportunity for the Indians to "pursue happiness in their own way," albeit in a barren land hundreds of miles away from everything they knew and the way of life they had established over many centuries. Either the white man or the red man had to go, and obviously it should be the red man. Coexisting with them was not possible: "They have neither the intelligence, the industry, the moral habits, nor the desire of improvement which are essential to any favorable change in

Figure 4.3 President Andrew Jackson framed the removal of Native Americans from their ancestral homes as "not only liberal but generous."

their condition." Removing the red man westward was "not only liberal, but generous," as the only alternative was "utter annihilation." There was no stopping progress; the Indians had already been eradicated from the North, and now "[t]he waves of population and civilization are rolling to the westward," as relentless and implacable as any natural force. By the end of the 1830s, over 100,000 Native Americans had been forced to migrate to desolate western lands on what became known as the "Trail of Tears," and many thousands of them had died of hunger, disease, exhaustion, and despair.[33]

This tragic tale vividly illuminates how group moral egoism often is justified by framing it in terms of what we may call here "the 3 Ns": *natural, normal*, and *necessary*. Framing behavior in this way absolves individuals within a group from any moral wrongdoing and makes the behavior seem inevitable rather than a matter of individual choice and responsibility. In fact, it is *not* engaging in the behavior that becomes questionable and subject to censure. If it's natural, normal, and necessary, why aren't you doing it?

Through socialization, cultures shape the imaginary realities of individuals, which reduces moral reflection. If everyone in the culture shares a similar group imaginary reality, there seem to be no good grounds to question it. It may never occur to you to question it. Group imaginary realities become represented in cultural institutions and rituals that condone behavior that might otherwise be regarded as wrong, even injuring or killing others. These group practices, like the individual behaviors, become regarded as natural, normal, and necessary.

Beginning in early childhood, people are socialized to embrace an imaginary reality that includes a moral worldview enshrining their group's ways as natural, normal, necessary—and therefore as good and right.[34] Through socialization children learn their culture's imaginary reality, which can be employed in the service of group moral egoism. The culture's imaginary reality functions as a filter that remembers and inflates positive experiences and achievements while downplaying, distorting, or silencing (and ultimately forgetting) episodes that might be construed as shameful and morally repugnant. The moral egoism of groups acts to defend a positive and flattering cultural imaginary reality, so that, in the aftermath of harm to another group, the acts are forgotten, distorted, justified, or even exalted, with the lead perpetrators regarded as heroes. Andrew Jackson is, after all, immortalized on the U.S. $20 bill.

Strategies of Group Moral Egoism

Most of the strategies of individual moral egoism presented earlier can be applied to group moral egoism as well.

Denial of Responsibility. It wasn't our intention to harm anyone. We were subject to desperate conditions, so we took desperate actions. Our leaders commanded us, so we really had no choice.

Denial of Harm. They are claiming much more damage than actually occurred. In fact, nobody really got hurt. They make it sound a lot worse than it actually was.

Condemning the Condemners. You don't have any right to be accusing us of doing something wrong. Your group has also done many bad things to other groups.

Just Deserts. We only gave them what they deserved. If we had not hurt them, they would have hurt us worse. We made sure that justice was done.

It Could Have Been Worse. We had the power to do much more damage than we actually did but chose not to. Don't we deserve some credit for that?

Redirection. This was one aberration under extreme conditions, but you are condemning us as a bad group for all time. You are ignoring how we have behaved well toward other groups for many years.

Appeal to Higher Loyalties. We were forced to act to protect our children/women/older people/other loved ones/way of life. If we had not acted, innocent people—*our* innocent people—would have been harmed. We were simply doing our duty.

Dehumanization. They are not truly human. They are more like vermin, insects, or other dangerous pests. So we exterminated them, just as you would exterminate any other pest. Their presence is akin to a disease, and the cure is to exile or exterminate them.

The psychology of collective violence, including war and genocide, would seem to be a stern test for a theory of moral egoism. Can group moral egoism be sustained even when there is abundant evidence that the perpetrator group has attempted to exterminate a victim group? The answer is unequivocally yes. The growing body of research on collective violence and genocide provides many vivid examples of the strategies of group moral egoism.

One example comes from research by Kjell Anderson on the attempted genocide of Tutsis by Hutus in Rwanda in the mid-1990s.[35] In radio broadcasts before the genocide began, Tutsis were dehumanized as cockroaches, snakes, and weevils (*Dehumanization*). Hutus were warned that Tutsis were coming to kill them; thus, killing Tutsis was framed as necessary, a form of group self-defense (*Just Deserts*). Killing Tutsis was also framed as morally right because it was a way of defending family, ethnic group, and country (*Appeal to Higher Loyalties*). In interviews following the genocide, perpetrators defended themselves as having little choice because they were within a hierarchy where killing Tutsis was expected and required (*Denial of Responsibility*). In fact, *not* being willing to take part in the killing would have been aberrant and subject to punishment. Many also defended their violent acts by claiming that their victims would have been killed by others if they had not done it, and that in fact their method of killing was more humane than what would have been done by others (*It Could Have Been Worse*). Similar strategies can be found in any case of collective violence or genocide (Figure 4.4).

Like individual moral egoism, group moral egoism provides a crucial advantage in competition with others. The fierce conviction that your group is right and the group that opposes you is wrong is stimulating and

Figure 4.4 The attacks of Hutus on Tutsis in Rwanda was one of many attempted genocides of the 20th century, all of them driven in part by group moral egoism.

motivating. It intensifies the emotions, and within groups it intensifies cohesion and commitment. There are many examples through history of groups that seemed to be at a disadvantage in conflict with other groups, lacking in numbers or resources, and yet they prevailed because their faith in the righteousness of their cause—their group moral egoism—was stronger than that of their adversaries. Both individual and group moral egoism thus confer power, and it is the advantage of this power that has made moral egoism selected for in human evolution and has made it a deep and enduring feature of the psychology of human nature.

Is Moral Egoism Humanity's Curse?

So far in this chapter, moral egoism has been portrayed as an especially dangerous aspect of imaginary realities. It shields us from an honest reckoning with our behavior, distorting moral reality to persuade us as individuals or groups that we are right and good, whatever we have done. At the individual level, moral egoism acts as a kind of self-righteous selfishness, allowing people to pursue their self-interest with zeal and yet feel good about it. This is a source of power: the person who pursues self-interest without guilt or scruple has an advantage in competition with someone whose motivation is constrained by conscience or empathy. Yet individual moral egoism also inflicts serious liabilities on human psychological and social functioning: arrogance, distortions of memory, corruption, and interpersonal conflict.

These liabilities are socially disruptive, so the tendency to individual moral egoism is typically discouraged or punished by cultural socialization. Suppressing individual moral egoism not only helps avoid its social disruptions but allows its emotional and motivational power to be redirected and applied to the moral egoism of the group. Group moral egoism, like individual moral egoism, confers power. It has given an advantage to some groups over others throughout human history, not only allowing group members to pursue the group's interest with unbridled intensity but promoting cohesion in a way that enhanced the group's effectiveness in competition with other groups.

For these reasons, group moral egoism has been a source of great pride and celebration throughout human history and a key component of groups' imaginary realities. The early Protestants led by Luther in persecuting the Jews, the early Americans zealously carrying out the ethnic cleansing of Native Americans, the Hutus running down the Tutsis in Rwanda, and many, many other groups before and after have exulted in their conviction that they were on the side of all that is good and right as they sought to dominate and even exterminate their less-than-human adversaries. They believed their group exemplified the highest human moral virtues: duty, loyalty, sacrifice, honor.

Of course, like other aspects of imaginary realities, to people on the outside of another group's moral egoism it looks quite different, not nearly so righteous and virtuous, especially with the distance of history. Today, with the rise of tolerance as a human value, we see many of these traditional "virtues" in a darker light: as justifications for racism, sexism, ethnocentrism, nationalism, and religious bigotry, often culminating in collective violence. All of these are expressions of group moral egoism. What looks like the highest good to a group enjoying moral egoism often looks like evil to the victims and to groups on the outside looking in.

Is moral egoism humanity's curse, then? Is there no way out of it? It appears from this description that moral egoism is such a deep part of our imaginary realities that it must find expression one way or another. Where individual moral egoism is suppressed, it finds expression instead in group moral egoism. The opposite may be true as well. As group moral egoism becomes weaker over time, individual moral egoism may become stronger.

There is evidence to support this conclusion. Arguably, group moral egoism is declining as intergroup tolerance ascends. Even though the 20th century was humanity's bloodiest, with more violent deaths from collective violence than in any previous century, the overall trend in recent centuries is a decline in violence.[36] Especially since the end of World War II, large-scale violence between groups, typically driven by group moral egoism, has waned. Higher levels of education may have made people more skeptical of outgroup stereotypes and prejudices. Numerous international organizations have been created for the explicit purpose of easing group conflict and promoting cooperation across borders, including the United Nations, the World Health Organization, the Organization for Economic Cooperation and Development, and regional alliances in Africa, Asia, Europe, Latin America, and North America. Globalization and its enhanced technologies of communication and transportation have spread a common base of information, ideas, and entertainments worldwide, leading many people to develop a multifaceted identity with one or more identities for their local environment as well as a global identity that allows them to feel comfortable with people of vastly different cultural backgrounds.[37] Group moral egoism thrives best in the dark, by limiting the information available to individuals in order to magnify group differences, but this goal is elusive in a globalized world where anyone with an internet connection has access to a limitless range of information and perspectives.

Yet history warns us not to be complacent and assume a future of tolerance and intergroup harmony is inevitable. The same optimistic sentiment was prevalent in the early 20th century, yet twice in the decades that followed group moral egoism fueled outbursts of world war that killed tens of millions of people. Today, although the internet provides access to an infinite range of information, it is also an abundant source of misinformation, used by individuals and groups to manipulate others and present group imaginary realities that distort social and political perceptions. In many cases people willfully close themselves into a finite information loop, sometimes composed of conspiracy theories and dehumanization of outgroups, and resist exposure to anything that would imperil their group moral egoism.

Despite the persistence of these perils, it seems clear that, overall, group moral egoism is waning. Does this mean that individual moral egoism is rising? It is difficult to say, as we do not have any direct historical measures of individual moral egoism that we could compare to the present. However, there is abundant evidence that individualism is on the rise worldwide, and individualism is a close cousin of individual moral egoism.[38] Similarly, it seems clear that the positive self-concept that is the basis of individual moral egoism gradually became one of the top goals of socialization in Western countries over the course of the 20th century, at the same time group moral egoism declined in power. The modern cultural value on the positive self-concept, and the socialization practices of cultures that hold the positive self-concept as a worthy ideal, result in higher individual moral egoism but dilute the moral egoism of the group. Instead, tolerance of group differences becomes highly valued, as individuals are taught to suppress any inclination to rank their own group's cultural beliefs and practices over any others. Recall how, among Middletown parents, already by 1978 tolerance ranked among the top two values they wanted their children to learn.

Still, the psychology of human nature is all about tendencies, not irrepressible instincts or reflexes. Maybe it is not true that moral egoism is such a strong part of the psychology of human nature that it is bound to be expressed one way or another, either as individual or as group moral egoism. Maybe it would be possible to change our individual and group perspectives so that both individual and moral egoism are reduced.

Is that something to be desired? Would we be better off without individual or group moral egoism? In some ways, certainly, but this may be a case of "be careful what you wish for." Group moral egoism fosters stereotypes of outgroups, prejudices, hatred, and sometimes collective violence, that is true. But it also gives people a sense of social identity, group belonging, security, and meaning.

As for individual moral egoism, there is no doubt it contributes to interpersonal conflict and makes intimate relationships more difficult and contentious. But is there a good side to it as well? We saw earlier in the chapter how individual moral egoism helps people cope in the aftermath of divorce. Individual moral egoism also confers a sense of personal power and motivates people to excel and outcompete their rivals. Is it possible that individual moral egoism is not just a source of interpersonal conflict but a motivator of individual achievement? Haven't many of the great innovators and artists and leaders of history held firmly to the belief "I know I am right" as others scoffed and even persecuted them? Martin Luther not only viciously excoriated the Jews; he also bravely exposed the corruptions of the Catholic Church, at great risk to himself. It may be that an unusually high level of moral egoism is a necessary ingredient of any high accomplishment in science, religion, politics, sports, or the arts. If that is true, less individual moral egoism could also mean less creativity, less cultural change, less intellectual dynamism, and fewer bold ideas. This is one of the many questions on moral egoism worth exploring.

5

Joy

Imagining Bliss

So far, the human propensity for creating imaginary realities has been portrayed mostly as a dangerous and deeply problematic feature of the psychology of human nature. As individuals and as groups, we inevitably distort our harsh and disagreeable reality into something more to our liking. This tendency provides a variety of benefits, from making our anxieties more manageable to stoking us with moral zeal against our competitors and promoting cooperation with others with whom we share a collective imaginary reality. However, it not only soothes our anxieties but creates new imaginary perils, and in stoking us with moral zeal it often leads us to be cruel and ruthless toward others, individually and collectively—and to feel good about it.

Joy would seem to be a type of imaginary reality that is unambiguously positive as a feature of human psychology. Alone among animals we have a remarkable ability to transform a mundane or threatening or burdensome reality into something delightful and pleasurable, strictly through a feat of imagination. When we are in discord with our physical or social reality, we have the capacity to imagine ourselves in joyful harmony with a different reality—with invisible beings and forces that are much friendlier than the ones actually in front of us, or with the promise of an afterlife that is full of myriad joys and eternally free of all stress and pain.

Yet, alas, nothing in our psychology is uncomplicated, even our joy. Yes, joy can transport us from dire and desperate conditions into a much more favorable psychological state, and it often both arises from and further strengthens our social bonds. But we also take joy in the suffering of our adversaries and find their joy painful to witness. Furthermore, we not only seek and celebrate joy, we sometimes fear it and avoid it or feel deeply guilty after pursuing it. All these variations will be examined in this chapter.

Imaginary Realities. Jeffrey Jensen Arnett, Oxford University Press. © Jeffrey Jensen Arnett (2026).
DOI: 10.1093/9780197817407.003.0005

Defining Joy

The word "joy" is used in a lot of different ways, so let me explain how I am defining it here. Joy is a uniquely human emotion. Animals experience pleasure, of course, and you could even say they experience something like happiness. Just like us they have *endorphins*, the hormonal foundation of pleasure and positive emotion, and they experience states that entail a rise in endorphins, so we can presume that they experience the feeling of happiness in a way that is at least analogous to our happiness. But joy is more than happiness. Joy includes intense happiness—*elation*, let's say—plus a feeling of *right relation* between ourselves and the world, a sense that there is an ideal fit between ourselves and the world around us at that moment. Joy requires a self-reflective identity in order to experience this sense of ideal relation between the self and the world. Only humans have a self-reflective identity, so only humans can experience joy.

Joy is *the elation of right relation*. The right relation that characterizes joy is "right" in the sense of being ideal; it is a deep feeling that our experience is ideal in that moment. In that state we imagine a perfect match between our identity and what we are experiencing. "This is great. Life is *good*. This could hardly be better." Joy is an intense, elated, but temporary state. It can last moments, minutes, even hours, but it is not perpetual. People vary in their readiness for joy and their opportunities for it, and consequently in the frequency of their joyful experiences.

Think of joy as being in the middle of a continuum of positive emotion, with quiet contentment on one end and ecstasy on the other. Joy is the sweet spot of positive emotion. It is different from contentment because it is more intense and more fleeting. It is different from ecstasy because ecstasy is at the peak of intensity, so intense that the person feels a loss of self, a temporary departure from the self. (The word "ecstasy" comes from a Greek word meaning "to stand outside of oneself.") In contrast, when we experience joy we are most deeply and serenely self-aware. We have a profound awareness of ourselves in right relation to the world around us—especially the social world but often the supernatural world as well, and sometimes the natural world.

Joy is highly pleasurable, but it is not defined by pleasure. In fact, as we shall see, it can even be experienced amid physical pain. It is highly pleasurable not because it triggers physical sensations of pleasure but because of the *meaning* we attribute to the emotional state. It is pleasurable because we experience heightened positive feelings when we perceive an ideal fit between who we are and the reality we imagine ourselves in.

Humans often experience joy even under conditions of stress, exertion, deprivation, and pain. We are such brilliant and gifted creators of imaginary realities that we can take even an experience of physical agony and give it a meaning that transforms it into a source of joy. This is uniquely human. Certainly if an experience is pleasurable other animals seek to repeat it or obtain more of it. But no other animal would willingly continue or repeat an experience that was physically aversive while redefining the experience as joyful. Every rat will keep pressing the bar that provides the pellet or the endorphin surge, but no rat would keep pressing the bar that delivers the electric shock and declare itself delighted with the result. Only we humans would do that. Only we humans have the capacity to create imaginary realities that transform the suffering of the world as it is into the joy of the world as we imagine it to be.

The Origins of Joy

Joy is evident from early in development, in loving attachments to those who care for us and in the delight we experience in being a member of a cohesive group of others we care about.

Foundations of Joy: Infant Attachments and Collective Effervescence

What is the most joyful, radiant smile you have ever seen? For me, that's easy: the smiles of my twins in their early years of life. Over 25 years later I still remember the thrill of their smiles, especially when I came in to greet them first thing in the morning or saw them after a time of separation. I remember vividly an episode that happened when my twins were about two years old. I was traveling quite frequently at that time, and I arrived home after being away for two or three days. I walked in the door and Miles, my son, was playing with toys in the front hallway about 10 feet away from the door. He looked up and saw me, and his face burst into a joyful grin. Immediately he sprang up and ran full speed toward me. When he got about three feet away he leaped off the ground into my arms, with full confidence that I would catch him, and I did. He melted into me with a full body embrace. That was a moment of pure joy for him, and for me, too (Figure 5.1).

There is a clear evolutionary reason for our joyful smiles: they inspire other people to love and care for us. There are few experiences more emotionally rewarding than being the recipient of a young child's smile. As an animal that is born helpless and has the longest period of learning and immaturity before we are able to obtain the resources we need for survival, we needed some way of appealing to others to love, protect, and care for us while we are most vulnerable. Joy is that way.

Within psychology, the framework that explains this infantile basis of joy is known as *attachment theory.*[1] British psychologist John Bowlby developed the theory in the 1960s to explain the emotional relations between infants and their mothers. He based it mainly on *ethology*, the study of animal behavior, noting how in all mammals the young are primed to stay close to their mother, not just for nourishment but for protection. In humans, our early joyful smiles are an effective way of eliciting others' love and care, and we especially display them during a reunion after a period of separation. Mothers have typically been our main attachment figures in infancy, because breastfeeding has been our main form of nourishment for the first year of

Figure 5.1 The emotional foundation of joy is in the reunion of a child with someone they love.

life, but we can become attached to anyone who provides loving care; common variations include older sisters and brothers, grandmothers, aunts, and fathers.

A healthy, secure attachment provides a prototype for our later social relations, and the joy of that attachment, especially in reunion episodes, provides the emotional foundation for our later experiences of joy. However, when we are young, the elation of right relation that defines joy is mostly emotional; we feel it, deeply, but we do not yet have the capacity to reflect on it. As we grow older joy becomes more cognitively complex. At first, joy is an unreflective burst of delight during reunion with a person we love and trust. But as we grow toward adulthood we elaborate joy so that it includes not just the emotion but also the cognitive, existential meaning of being in right relation to the world.

The other major emotional component of the foundation of joy is the positive feeling we experience in being part of a cohesive group. In the 19th century the sociologist Émile Durkheim called this feeling *collective effervescence.*[2] Durkheim formed this concept in seeking to understand tribal rituals involving music and dance from a sociological perspective. In his account, these rituals serve to promote group cohesion and collective action. During group rituals, participants experience "emotional contagion" as they influence and intensify each other's emotional states.

I love the term *collective effervescence*, but I would frame it in a more psychological way: as a form of joy that promotes group identity, trust, and unity. It enhances the emotional connections among group members. It is built from the same emotional material as infant–caregiver attachment, including love, trust, and social acceptance. In fact, its emotional basis is derived from that original infant attachment. Like individual attachments, collective effervescence becomes more psychologically complex with age, and in adolescence and adulthood it is typically rooted in a shared imaginary reality. Its evolutionary function at the group level is clear: it promotes coordination, cooperation, cohesion, and conformity, resulting in more effective group action, including in competition or conflict with other groups.

Think of examples from your own life when you have felt the joy of collective effervescence. Nearly all of us have this experience from time to time, and there is usually a shared imaginary reality that is the basis of it. Team sports participation, coordinated dances, and group musical performances are examples that many people experience. All religions have group rituals of some kind, and most people in the world participate in religious rituals at least occasionally. In some religions these rituals are solemn and subdued, but in some they are joyful and exuberant and bubble with collective effervescence. We also have secular rituals such as graduations marking educational achievements and parades marking national holidays. These, too, are often a combination of the solemn and the joyful. Weddings are another good example. Typically at a wedding people gather together everyone they love the most (as well as, admittedly, some they don't love at all but happen to be related to). The reception that follows is often a memorable occasion of collective effervescence.

There are group activities that are less ritualized but are golden opportunities for experiencing the joy of collective effervescence. Rock concerts, sporting events, and dancing to music are examples that many people experience today. More broadly, any party or meal where people whom you love are gathered together can inspire collective effervescence. The joy of collective effervescence can be boisterous and exuberant, but it can also be felt while enjoying a meal and conversation with a small circle of people you love. Remember, the essence of joy is that it is a delighted sense of right relation to the world. You can feel that dancing and singing exuberantly with others, but you can also feel it in a quiet gathering of family or friends.

Do Rats Laugh?

Let's return to the question of whether humans uniquely experience joy. To start we can note that humans are the only ape that smiles. Other primates bare their teeth, but to express fear or aggression or submission, not as a positive emotion. In contrast, we smile to express joy, love, and affiliation, beginning when we are two to three months old and continuing ever after. We are, quite literally, built for joy, uniquely among animals.

Play is another place to examine the uniqueness of human joy, as humans frequently experience joy in their various experiences of play. Are we also the only animal that plays? Most researchers on animal behavior think not.[3] Among mammals, especially young mammals, there is frequently some form of "rough-and-tumble" play that entails wrestling and perhaps light biting but without injury or breaking the skin. One researcher on rats describes this kind of play among rats as "rambunctious shenanigans," adding that it is accompanied by chirps that "reflect positive emotional feelings."[4] Chimpanzee juveniles play chase games and tickle each other. Rats also apparently like to be tickled. Similarly, rough-and-tumble play and chase games are among the most frequent types of play among human children, and they like to be tickled, too.

So we can probably say that other animals play, if we define "play" broadly in terms of its resemblance to similar human play activities. But do they experience joy? This seems more doubtful if we are thinking of joy as an elated emotional state that includes a meaningful sense of right relation to the world. I think there is a fair amount of anthropomorphism in the way researchers describe animal play. Even calling it "play" is questionable, as this assumes that animals, too, are engaged in activities that are primarily for the sake of enjoyment and delight, not for any practical purpose. But animal play is highly practical. Rough-and-tumble play and chase games are both ways of attempting to assert dominance. Assertion of dominance underlies the human forms of these games, too, but the laughter and delight that are part and parcel of games among human children are different than what seems to occur among other animals; in humans they seem to reflect joy.

Sure, some rudimentary form of joy exists among animals. We are animals, too, and we evolved from earlier animals just as today's other animals did, so of course there are similarities between us and them, especially between us and our closest primate relatives. But joy is made of a combination of emotional, social, cognitive, and imaginary reality components that exist only in us. Only humans experience joy as the elation of right relation.

Varieties of Joy

Throughout our species' history and into the present, we have proven ourselves able to tap joy from a wide variety of sources, everything from eating and drinking to sports and sex. Here our focus will be on the forms of joy that have connections to imaginary realities.

The Joy of Imaginary Realities: I Was Blind, but Now I See

Our imaginary realities help us make sense of everything, and the feeling they provide for us of having a secure place in the world sometimes inspires the elation of right relation that constitutes joy, especially in the context of rituals celebrating our shared beliefs. Through nearly all of our species' history we have lived in relatively small groups, ranging from a few dozen to a couple of hundred, in what anthropologists call "small-scale societies."[5] In small-scale societies there is only one imaginary reality that everyone shares. Children are taught to embrace it from their early months of life, not just through explicit teaching but through observing and taking part in cultural practices.[6] Adults are guided by the collective imaginary reality as they go about their daily lives because it sets guidelines for how they should behave in relation to others. On special occasions, ritual celebrations display the imaginary reality, and the joy of taking part in those celebrations deepens people's attachments to it.

In the larger and more complex societies where nearly all people live today, most are aware that there is more than one possible imaginary reality. Although people are typically taught an imaginary reality from infancy, in a pluralistic society there are many alternative imaginary realities in addition to the dominant one. Pressure for conformity to embrace the dominant imaginary reality is not as severe as it has been in the human past, and some people find that it does not resonate with them emotionally and existentially. If they find an alternative imaginary reality that provides the ideological key they have been seeking, the result is typically a feeling of great joy.

The Christian religion is the best known for inspiring this kind of joy because it has been an evangelical religion from its founding, seeking converts who will embrace its truths and promising great joy in return. From the story of Paul being struck blind on the road to Damascus to the present, the Christian narrative is replete with conversions and reports of being "born again." The term "born again" is quite fascinating and apt in this context, as it implies becoming a new person with a new identity as one's previous imaginary reality is displaced by the Christian worldview. But it is not only Christianity that has inspired the experience of revelation, of suddenly becoming convinced that you have found the key to all of the most important personal and collective existential questions. Reports of joyful revelation similar to Christian born-again experiences can be found in accounts of "conversions" to political ideologies such as Marxism, cults ranging from Scientology to QAnon, and even psychoanalysis.[7] Clearly, we have a species potentiality for the psychological experience of conversion to an ideology, and the discovery and embrace of a new imaginary reality is nearly always accompanied by a rare and sublime joy.

The Joy of Music

Recently an extraordinary archaeological discovery was announced: a flute, made of bone, 30,000 years old. It looked remarkably like a flute you might see today. How moving to find evidence of humans playing music so long ago! Long before we invented the plow or the wheel or the crossbow, we were inventing ways to make music. Music almost certainly goes back much farther into our past. Researchers on language regard singing as a likely "protolanguage," a way of communicating that predates communicating with words.[8] Even before we were speaking to each other, we were singing to each other.

Music serves a variety of functions. It is an excellent mnemonic, allowing us to preserve group history and traditions and pass them through the generations. It promotes group cohesion, as we gather to play, sing, and listen together. And almost always, making music means making joy. That joy is functional, too. Music promotes collective effervescence, and the joy we feel in sharing music together enhances the bonds between us, including feelings of trust and mutual obligation and shared beliefs. It causes us to feel the elation of right relation to each other as well as to the outer world we face together. Music is a human universal, and in every human society it is a joyful part of group festivals and celebrations.[9]

Evidence of our joyful responsiveness to music appears early. Even in the womb we respond to music, moving to melodies. Babies are born grooving; across cultures, infants and toddlers spontaneously move to a rhythm. Infants are soothed by familiar songs, and music therapy for preterm infants enhances their physical health, helping them breathe better.[10] Adults often speak to infants in a musical way, with exaggerated intonations and variations in pitch, and this "infant-directed speech" promotes language development. All over the world, music is part of children's joyful play. In her book *Songs in Their Heads: Music and Its Meaning in Children's Lives*, Patricia Sheehan Campbell observes, "Children think aloud through music. They socialize, vent emotions, and entertain themselves through music. Their bodies stretch, bend, step, hop, and skip in rhythmic ways, while their melodic voices rise and fall. . . . It is almost as if children exude music."[11] Throughout life, research shows that people use music to regulate their moods, especially to lift themselves up from a low mood and to enhance and promote joy.

Music often sounds joyful, but of course it can be sad or angry, too. Even here, however, joy may be the end result. Music can have a *cathartic effect*, intensifying negative feelings like sadness or anger and then washing them out, so that afterward we feel cleansed and renewed. Early in my career, I did an extensive study of fans of heavy metal music, "metalheads" as they called themselves.[12] I found the music aversive and depressing, so I was intrigued by their devotion to it and wanted to know why. The most unexpected and fascinating finding of my research was that the music had a cathartic effect: they listened to it especially when they were angry (and they were angry *a lot*), and it had the effect of *calming them down*. They felt better afterward—definitely less unhappy than before, and sometimes even joyful. I went to many heavy metal concerts in the course of my research, and they were always festivals of collective effervescence, replete with music-inspired joy.

A key part of their joy in listening to metal was a shared imaginary reality with other metalheads. This shared imaginary reality was cynical verging on nihilistic, but it was somehow made joyful for them in knowing they were not alone; they were part of a vast community of other metalheads who shared this grim view of the adult world and its institutions.

Party Time: The Joy of Festivals

As part of our construction of imaginary realities, we imagine a structure for time that it does not actually have. The yearly changes in the climate and the length of days and nights are continuous, but we imagine them into distinct seasons: spring, summer, autumn, winter. Our individual development is continuous, but we imagine it as divided into distinct life stages—infancy, childhood, youth, adulthood, old age—and often mark the transitions from one life stage to the next.[13] Each year we mark another "birthday," although we are little different the day before or the day after, as a way of drawing attention to the passage of time and the more notable changes that take place from one year to the next.

Not only do we imagine time as divided into discrete chunks, but our cultural creativity invents joyful festivals to celebrate the chronological milestones we invent: spring festivals and May Days, harvest festivals, days honoring saints and gods and God and ancestors and other cultural heroes. Perhaps the most remarkable feat of imagination of all these festivals is the tradition of celebrating the winter solstice, the darkest day of the year.

(Long before it became the Christmas holiday in Christian lands, it was a winter solstice festival more broadly.) Imagine what this time of year has been like for nearly all of human history. The world was lit only by fire, so it was dark for the great majority of each 24-hour period. Food was often scarce; whatever store of root vegetables you had set aside at harvest time was dwindling by now, and your hunting expeditions yielded less and less as animals either hibernated or migrated or otherwise made themselves scarce. And it was cold! Unless you lived near the equator, by the time of the winter solstice you had been cold a lot, with only the fire to warm you, and you couldn't spend all day huddled around it: there was always work to be done.

Our collective cultural response to this dire predicament? Let's have a party! After all, if it is the darkest day of the year, that means that every day for the next half-year will be longer! Just like that, what might seem like the worst time of the year becomes an occasion for joy.

Festivals have been present in all eras in all societies, and they have a remarkably consistent set of ingredients: music and dance, special foods and drinks (served in abundance), costumes and bodily decorations (Figure 5.2).[14] Crowds gather for the festival in much greater numbers than

Figure 5.2 Every society has joyful celebrations and festivals that express collective effervescence. Here, revelers celebrate the annual Carnival festival in Brazil.

during everyday life. There is a pause from normal work activities—although someone has to make the food and drinks, and the preparation of the music and dance performances and the costumes and bodily decorations may occur for weeks or even months before the event. The festival is eagerly anticipated long before it occurs, and collective effervescence rises to a peak during the event itself.

Sometimes the drinks are intoxicating and there are other mind-altering substances. Sometimes festivals include competitions, especially among the young, of beauty or strength or games or sports. Sometimes popular imaginary realities are mocked and there are role reversals, the elites dressing like the common people and the common people mocking the elites—crowning a "king of fools," for example. More generally, there is often a widespread sense that typical norms and rules are suspended or reversed. Sometimes this leads to outbursts of violence and destruction and sexual license, and at times elites have suspended or abolished festivals in part for this reason. But more commonly, festivals take place in a spirit of joy, and the suspension of normal rules of conduct occurs within prescribed limits.

Live sports events are a modern form of festival, complete with feasting, drinking intoxicants, costumes and body decorations, and often music and dancing as part of the show. You can get a better view of the actual sports competition by staying home and watching it on TV, but the live sports event allows for joyful participation in the festival. We take joy in marveling at the skills of people who have honed their athletic gifts to the farthest extreme of human abilities, far beyond what we are capable of ourselves. Our ability to empathize, to imagine ourselves in the place of others, gives us a sense of what it would be like to perform those marvelous feats.

But imaginary realities also make a substantial contribution to the joy we take in watching live sports. Sports competitions are often structured around teams, and we can attach ourselves emotionally and socially to our team so that when they win, we win, too. The collective imaginary realities we construct in our allegiances to our favorite teams are often morally tinged—our team is not just better than yours athletically; it is better morally. We have group virtues, such as hard work, shared sacrifice, and group commitment, that your team lacks—we *deserve* to win. Our ingroup–outgroup allegiances are provoked by team sports competitions, and when our ingroup is triumphant, we feel that joyful triumph, too, the pleasure of being part of the dominant group and subduing those in another group. Watching sports competitions, we feel a far greater emotional intensity than we feel in the course of our normal everyday lives—anxiety and sorrow, sometimes, but there is also the ever-present possibility of joy, of an outburst of collective effervescence.

The Joy of Sex? It's Complicated

There is no doubt that sexual activity is a source of physical pleasure for humans, as it is for other mammals. If it were not, none of our species would have lasted long. There are specific parts of our brains devoted to sexual pleasure, and our nerve endings are concentrated in our genitalia to make them ultra-sensitive for responding to sexual stimulation.

But is sex *joyful*? That is a more complicated question. As with everything human, our response to sex is not merely physical. We also make sex part of our imaginary realities: it is moral and existential, and reflecting on our participation in it (or not) affects our identity, our sense of who we are and what our life means. Crucially, how we *think* about sex—the expectations, the fantasies, the meanings we apply to sexual desire and experience—is even more important to sexual joy than our physiological responses. Part of our ability to create imaginary realities is that we always add layers of imagination and invention onto our physical experiences, including our sexual experiences. People can experience an intense orgasm and yet experience no joy, and they can experience no orgasm at all and yet find a sexual experience joyful.

Above all, sex, like everything human, takes place through the structure and filter and lens of our imaginary realities. To illuminate this, let's look more closely at the cultural contrast to American views of sexuality that can be found in the Hindu cultural tradition in India.[15] In the traditional Hindu life stage model, young adulthood is considered to be the life stage of *jouvana*, a word that literally means "sexually active." The more sexually active the young couple is, the more likely that they will soon produce children, and having children is considered to be the central meaning and purpose of marriage. So you could say that sexual joy during this stage of life is encouraged. Next, however, comes the midlife stage of "forest dweller." This stage is marked when the first grandchild is born, which for most Indians takes place in their 40s. As a forest dweller, a person is supposed to begin relinquishing attachments to the things of this world and gradually turn to religious life and the pursuit of spiritual purity. For Hindus, this search for a higher spiritual life includes renunciation of sexuality. In fact, even before the first grandson is born, midlife sexuality ceases if the oldest child is a son, because Hindus believe it is wrong for parents and children to be having sexual relations within the same household and sons typically bring their new wife to their parents' home to live. In sum, there is sexual joy in India, but for Indians who are Hindu it is restricted to the young adult years, and even during those years only when the woman is neither pregnant nor nursing; sex is taboo under those conditions.

So we modern Westerners are the lucky ones, right? In Western countries today, our cultural beliefs celebrate the joy of sex throughout adulthood. Joyful sex is widely considered to be a healthy part of a loving intimate relationship, for women and men alike. Most women will become pregnant only once or twice, maybe three times, beginning around age 30, leaving many years before and after for sexual enjoyment without reproduction. We have a wide variety of effective ways of avoiding pregnancy, which makes it possible for us to have sex sheerly for the joy of it, more than it has ever been possible before. We celebrate (or at least allow) not only heterosexual enjoyment but a wide range of other ways of pursuing sexual joy: same-sex relations, self-stimulation, polyamory, pornography, and more.

Whether all of this makes sex more *joyful* is a more difficult question to answer. I would say it probably does. It matters, greatly, that we have largely lifted the burden of guilt from sex and that we now, culturally, encourage and celebrate sexual joy. It matters greatly that we have managed to decouple sex from reproduction so that we are able to enjoy sex simply for the joy of it. But—complicated psychological creatures that we are—we have also raised our expectations for the contribution sexual joy will make to our overall joie de vivre, and that can be a daunting expectation to fulfill.

Darker Shades of Joy

Even for a topic like joy, it is important to reckon with the aspects of it that are not especially flattering to us as a species, and to examine the role that imaginary realities play in these twisted forms of joy. We take joy in many wonderful things, from our responses to music and dance to our collective participation in festivals. But we also take joy in many things that have a more ambiguous value, from harm to others to self-suppression. Furthermore, the people who have attained power in large and complex societies have sometimes been devoted to killing joy, or at least controlling it and suppressing it except in state-approved (and ultimately joyless) ways. Now we turn our attention to those darker shades of joy.

The Joy of (Others') Pain: Schadenfreude and Sadism

One long-recognized form of joy is *schadenfreude*, a German word literally meaning "taking joy (*freude*) in the harm (*schaden*) occurring to others." There has been a substantial amount of theory and research on schadenfreude, especially in recent years, and scholars agree that its roots are in a combination of competitive insecurity, malicious envy, and morality.[16] We feel schadenfreude especially when something bad happens to someone we view as being in competition with us for resources or status, especially when that person is someone we envy and we have been hoping they would suffer misfortune. Above all, schadenfreude is moral, in the sense that it is typically provoked by a belief that the harmed persons deserved what they got.

Schadenfreude fits well with the concept of moral egoism presented in the previous chapter. Moral egoism is our tendency to twist our evaluations of moral issues and situations so that we come out on top. We are prone to seeing ourselves or our group as in the right and the other person or group as wrong, irrespective of the objective facts of the event. Schadenfreude is part of the emotional substructure of moral egoism. When something bad happens to someone we already do not like and feel ourselves to be in conflict or competition with, this deepens our sense that we are in right relation to the world and our adversary is in the wrong.[17] The moral order of things seems to be operating just as it should, by seeing to it that those opposed to us experience misfortune. We feel ourselves in right relation to the moral order, and that feeling of right relation is experienced as joy. Part of our moral training in all societies is to be considerate of the feelings of others and empathize with them when they suffer. But schadenfreude, like the moral egoism that is the basis for it, allows us to compete ruthlessly with others and feel good about it, sustained by the belief that they deserve the bad things that are happening to them and we deserve to be the beneficiaries of the moral order's rewards.

Just as there is group moral egoism as well as individual moral egoism, there is a group form of schadenfreude as well as a personal form.[18] When bad things happen to a group with whom our ingroup is in conflict or competition, we feel that the moral order is operating as it should, and we feel a joyful sense of right relation and triumph. Schadenfreude contributes emotional fuel to group moral egoism. We tend to see the suffering of outgroups as natural, normal, and necessary, a testament to the vitality of the moral order of the universe. We can experience schadenfreude when they suffer because it is clear to us that they deserve their misfortune, and in any case they do not seem fully human to us, or at least not as human as we are.

Sadism is related to schadenfreude, but it is more active, as it involves taking pleasure from inflicting pain on others, not just enjoying the harm that occurs to them without our involvement. Some people can enjoy causing pain to others if their moral egoism is deep enough for them to believe the others deserve it, but for most people this would be too high a bar for their moral egoism to leap. Again, nearly all of us are taught as part of our early socialization not to hurt other people and to empathize with them when they suffer. This basic foundation of socialization can be twisted into sadistic joy only if moral egoism is raised to an unusually high level or if the deliverer of pain has an unusually low ability to empathize.

For both schadenfreude and sadism, imaginary realities assist us in overcoming whatever qualms we have about experiencing joy inspired by the suffering of others. We may believe, for example, that God or the gods are the ones delivering the suffering, which confirms that the sufferers deserved what they got. Or, even without gods, we may believe that there is a "just world" moral order that the sufferers have violated, and so they must be punished, inevitably. Through these kinds of beliefs, our empathic tendency to wish others well and have concern when they are suffering can be evaded.

The Joy of Not Enjoying: Self-Denial and Masochism

We are born with a readiness to learn the ways of a culture, and over the course of our early years we learn what is allowed and what is not allowed, what is praised and what is punished, what the boundaries are of our cultural requirements. At first we learn self-restraint, to avoid doing things that are disapproved. Gradually we internalize cultural limits so that we attain *self-regulation*, guided by a moral framework and a conscience, enabling us to follow cultural rules without much thinking about them.

There is not much pain in following the guidance of self-regulation, but there is not much joy in it either. However, if we take self-regulation to an extreme, willfully going beyond what our culture requires, to *self-denial*, this can sometimes be experienced as joyful.[19] There is often an elevated status that goes along with it. Others look upon those who are voluntarily and willfully reducing their animal desires for sex or food or physical comfort beyond the normal restraints and marvel, even though most have little interest in following that severe example. The ascetics themselves feel a sense of joy and triumph in it, both from their elevated status and from showing themselves, too, that they are capable of feats of self-denial that most people are not. Self-denial is often perceived as a victory over our animal nature in favor of something higher and better, as a way of declaring, "Look! I am no mere animal. I have triumphed over those crude desires and raised myself to a higher plane." At the extreme, their humility becomes a kind of vanity.

Self-denial is typically motivated by imaginary realities. Across cultures, paragons of self-denial have often been religious figures, sometimes religious heroes. According to anthropologists, shamans in small-scale societies often perform self-denial of sex and food in order to demonstrate their special status and their rare access to supernatural powers.[20] In several major religious traditions—Buddhism, Hinduism, Catholicism, and Islam—exceptional piety has often been demonstrated by giving up or severely restricting sexual activity, by reducing and narrowing the range of food intake, and by a willingness to accept physical discomfort or pain: extremes of hot or cold, sleeping on a hard floor, or wearing clothes that are threadbare and inadequate for warmth or comfort. The ascetics are motivated by believing that supernatural figures or forces endorse or require these sacrifices and will reward them.

Two examples of the joy of privation in the Christian tradition are "fasting saints," mostly women, and flagellants, mostly men. Extreme fasting, to the point of eating barely enough to stay alive, was associated with piety among Christian women for about 500 years beginning in the 12th century.[21] Young women who engaged in extreme fasting often gained great fame and were regarded by their contemporaries with reverence and awe, and some were even deemed to be saints (Figure 5.3). The flagellant movement flourished in Italy and Germany in the 13th and 14th centuries.[22] Flagellants roamed from town to town, whipping themselves bloody to the rhythm of religious songs, sometimes veering past joy to ecstatic visions—the sky opening to reveal heaven, with Jesus or the Virgin Mary beckoning.

Participants in religious privations often describe the experience joyfully, claiming to find delight in the willing embrace of discomfort and pain as an offering to their gods. But to a 21st-century ear, the kinds of extreme

Figure 5.3 Catherine of Sienna became renowned as a fasting saint in 14th century Italy.

self-denial that made a person a candidate for religious veneration a few centuries ago sound like masochism: unhealthy, probably pathological, a symptom of mental illness. Yet even today, for those who hold an imaginary reality belief that frames their self-inflicted suffering as a gift to their deity, masochism can be experienced as joy, as the elation of right relation, even though it may seem pathologically misguided to those who do not share that belief.

Killjoys: Denying Joy to Others

Joy is perhaps the peak kind of human experience. When we think of the best, most wonderful moments of our lives, we think of those times when we felt an elated sense of right relation to the world. Joy is often social, and our own joy is enhanced by sharing it with those we love. Yet there is also a long human tradition of feeling threatened, angered, and appalled by the joy of others—especially if we regard them as unlike us or opposed to us. There is even a German word that is the counterpart to schadenfreude: *gluckschmerz*, feeling bad about others' joy.[23]

The psychological basis of schadenfreude applies to gluckschmerz as well, in particular their common roots in moral egoism, at both the individual and the group level. At the individual level we are in competition with others for status and resources. Schadenfreude feels good because when bad things happen to others who compete with us we move ahead of them in the race; when good things happen to them we feel correspondingly bad because they have moved ahead of us. The basis of these emotions is moral; when bad things happen to our rivals we feel joy because they got what they deserved, but when good things happen to them we feel disheartened and diminished because the moral order is out of whack. They were the beneficiaries of good fortune even though they did not deserve it (or at least did not deserve it as much as we do).

At the group level, the joyous celebrations of outgroups seem potentially threatening to our ingroup. Their apparent good fortune and good spirits imply they are successfully competing against us. Just as at the individual level, we feel they cannot possibly deserve such favor, so the moral order seems disrupted. Moreover, outgroup ways of expressing joy are unfamiliar to us, being based on an imaginary reality different from ours, so their celebrations seem strange and repugnant, the *wrong way* of being joyful. Like us, they may celebrate with music, dance, feasts, costumes, and bodily decorations, but theirs are the *wrong* forms of music, dance, and so on. Our forms of collective effervescence are venerable and beautiful; yours are crude, appalling, even disgusting.

There are many examples of this response in the accounts of Europeans who witnessed ritual expressions of group joy as they roamed and ransacked the world in the 18th and 19th centuries.[24] A Jesuit missionary in the late 19th century described the celebratory festivals of the Yup'ik people in Alaska by concluding, "In general their superstitions are a fearful worship of the devil. They indulge profusely in performances and feasts to please their dead but in fact to please and corrupt themselves, in dancing and banqueting."[25] For another example, here is Charles Darwin's bemused response to observing the aboriginal people of western Australia making music and dancing:

> The dancing consisted in their running either sideways or in Indian file into an open space, and stamping the ground with great force as they marched together. Their heavy footsteps were accompanied with a kind of grunt, by beating their clubs and spears together, and by various other gesticulations, such as extending their arms and wriggling their bodies. It was a most rude, barbarous scene, and, to our ideas, without any sort of meaning.[26]

This kind of befuddled, contemptuous response to the rituals of an outgroup is unsurprising in light of group moral egoism. We nearly always see the customs of other cultural groups as inferior to our own because they are based on an imaginary reality that is different and therefore strange and repellent. But the question remains: Why should there be killjoys, even within our cultural ingroup, seeking to suppress our own cultural traditions of expressing group joy? Our species' history is replete with such killjoys. One of the most notorious was Girolamo Savonarola, the monk who led an anti-joy crusade for the Catholic Church in Europe during the late 15th century, claiming that the Apocalypse was imminent and now was the time to show our readiness for it by burning all worldly inspirations of enjoyment. The culmination of the crusade was the "Bonfire of the Vanities" in 1497, when a huge mass of joy-inducing objects was set aflame in a public square in Florence: art, books, costumes, and cosmetics.

It may be tempting to dismiss this as a twisted example of the unique killjoy tendencies of Christianity, but similar events have occurred in other religious traditions, East and West, as well as in secular regimes such as the French revolutionaries of the 18th century and the 20th-century fascists and communists. Why? Certainly at the heart of it is the goal of asserting one imaginary reality and squelching a threatening alternative. Another common thread appears to be that group joy can be unruly and uncontrollable and can therefore seem dangerous to those who hold power. On some occasions, festival celebrations have spilled over into popular revolts; today we need only think of the looting and vandalism that frequently accompany the celebration of a major sports victory for ready examples. To authorities it can seem safer to simply discourage all expressions of group joy except those tightly controlled by the authorities.

The Joy of Overcoming Pain: The "Ordinary Magic" of Resilience

Joy as I have defined it in this chapter is an intense but temporary feeling. We experience it when we feel the elation of the just-right fit between our identity and the moment, and then the moment passes. However, it could also be observed that people vary in their readiness for joy, some feeling it frequently and easily and others rarely, only under special circumstances.

There are probably inherited, genetically based individual differences in our readiness to feel joy, just as we vary in our readiness for sadness or aggression. However, our readiness for joy can also be based on the kinds of experiences we have had in the past. In general, people who have grown up in a loving, stable family are likely to have a greater readiness for joy than people who have not. Remember, the early experience of delighted reunion with a loving attachment figure is the emotional prototype of joy, and if that prototype is defective or shattered, joy is harder to come by ever after.

Nevertheless, our creativity in forming personal imaginary realities is sometimes marvelous enough to allow us to overcome a confusing and painful childhood and turn it into a joyful hero story of how the confusion and pain were overcome. Psychologists call this *resilience*, defined as good outcomes despite bad conditions. Sometimes "good outcomes" are marked by reaching notable milestones (such as graduating from college or holding a stable job), sometimes by internal conditions (such as good mental health), and sometimes by the absence of notable problems (such as early pregnancy, homelessness, substance abuse, or criminal behavior). People who are resilient do not necessarily become high achievers who have some kind of extraordinary ability. More often they display what resilience researcher Ann Masten calls the "ordinary magic" of being able to function reasonably well despite being faced with unusually difficult circumstances.[27]

One of the rewards of resilience is joy. People who have generally experienced good conditions and good fortune throughout their early development are usually reasonably happy with their life as an adult, although of course there is variation depending on how their adult life goes. But people who have experienced deprivation or abuse as children and adolescents and nevertheless go on to have a successful adult life often experience a deeper joy because of the distance they have come from their early suffering. Enduring a long dark night of the soul makes the rising of the sun not just routine but joyful, because you had good reason to fear it might not come up again. A key part of resilience is transforming the personal narrative so that early suffering is viewed not just as something that was survived but as something that was *necessary* in order for the person to become who they are today.[28] Their early years went badly wrong, but they achieved the capacity for the elation of right relation by transforming how they think about their early years. Resilient adults mostly do not regret the harsh conditions of their childhood, but rather embrace their trials as the necessary fire to forge the stronger person they have become as a consequence. A crucial element in this interpretation is an imaginary reality that serves as its foundation; God had a plan for me, for example, or the turn my life took at a crucial moment was "meant to be." It can inspire great joy to realize that all of your pain was part of a plan; everything, even the worst parts, happened for a reason.

Let's end this chapter on joy with a case study of the joy of resilience, one clearly connected to the embrace of a new imaginary reality, from my decades of research on emerging adults.

Bridget, age 23, endured a childhood that included physical abuse, emotional abuse, alcoholism, bitter conflict, and eventual estrangement from both her parents. "My family is the role model for the dysfunctional family," she said wistfully. When her parents were not abusing each other, they abused Bridget and her younger sister. "Mom was good at verbal abuse, and Dad was good at the physical. Of course, the verbal was worse." Bridget's mind still resonates with all the harsh things her mother told her as she was growing up. "You're ugly. You're fat. You'll never have any friends. You're stupid."

How did Bridget emerge from this nightmare to find joy? One key was the development of her religious faith, which has been found to be an important protective factor in studies of resilience. She started attending a church because a boy she had a crush on went there, and from this casual beginning it became a refuge during her otherwise painful high school years:

> I wonder now what my life would have been like had I not had this positive influence. All throughout high school, because of that church group I was always around happy people, people that had fun with their lives, people that really enjoyed living. I am so close to some families at church that just really helped me out. They give this unconditional love. That's something I still don't understand, how people that barely knew me could give me unconditional love because of Jesus, so much more than my own parents.

In emerging adulthood, not only has Bridget separated herself from destructive family influences but she has also created a narrative of her past family experiences that interprets her suffering as something that has built her up rather than torn her down. "There's been a lot of pain and a lot of hurt, but I've really grown from it," she says. She sees her experiences, even the bad ones, as an essential part of her journey. "It's made me the person who I am today. It all happens for a reason."

Bridget's career ambitions are a work in progress, like many people her age, but she thinks she may wish to be a high school teacher. She's more certain about her desire to have a husband and children. Witnessing her parents' awful relationship has made her cautious about marriage, but not cynical: "I love the idea of falling in love and having someone to share your life with. I think I'd be ready for that if I found the right person. But I'm not going to rush it. I'm not going to settle for anything less than I deserve." She envisions providing her own children with a joyful family life much different from her own. "A real loving household. Open communication. No violence. I will never strike a child."

Although Bridget's life right now is uncertain, one thing she is certain about is that the future she imagines is bright. "I look at what's happened in the last two years of my life, and it's changed so much that I can't possibly see what's going to happen in ten years. It'll be pretty exciting, I'm sure."

6
Humor
Reinforcing and Puncturing Imaginary Realities

Like joy, humor is psychologically complex. What we find funny is highly varied, just as what we find joyful is highly varied. In the same way that we can find joy in our love for others and our festive celebrations as well as in the suffering of others and even ourselves, so we can use humor to inflate and fortify the delusions represented by imaginary realities—but also to expose them as delusions and destroy them.

Humor is not just a source of mirth and fun that harmlessly lightens up our days. It has many purposes, but above all humor in human relations is a way of using imaginary realities to exercise power. Specifically, it is a method used by ingroups to invoke and intensify the imaginary reality of the superiority of the ingroup in contrast to the hopelessly stupid, contemptible, loathsome outgroup.

Across cultures and over millennia, the most popular type of humor is disparagement humor, which supports ingroup–outgroup stereotypes by ridiculing the deficiencies of outgroups and laughing at their suffering.[1] This kind of humor serves the purpose of reinforcing the imaginary reality that everyone in our group is superior to everyone in your group, by virtue of the fact that they are in our group. Disparagement humor also dehumanizes the outgroup and thereby justifies treating them as the subhumans they are.

Yet we use humor not only to support imaginary realities but to subvert them.[2] We are psychologically constructed to learn and embrace imaginary realities, at both the individual and the group level. However, clever and complicated creatures that we are, we sometimes see through the illusions we are being taught and recognize them for what they are. When we do, humor is the key toolbox we use for puncturing imaginary realities and exposing them as false. Across cultures and times, there is great fun to be found in mocking the lies and vanity and stupidity of the people who hold power

Imaginary Realities. Jeffrey Jensen Arnett, Oxford University Press. © Jeffrey Jensen Arnett (2026).
DOI: 10.1093/9780197817407.003.0006

over us. Thus, in this chapter there will be two main sections, the first on *disparagement humor* and the second on *subversive humor.*

Just as in the joy chapter there were many aspects of it that were not likely to induce joy in the reader, so in the humor chapter there will be a lot that you will not find the least bit humorous. The disparagement humor section, especially, will make for some tough reading, because it shows how humor is used as a harsh and ruthless weapon to reinforce imaginary realities about one group's superiority over another. But not to worry, the section on subversive humor will contain plenty of examples of witty attacks on imaginary realities that richly deserved to be subverted and on the liars who were puffing them up and attempting to deceive.

Disparagement Humor

We have previously seen, especially in the chapter on moral egoism, how deeply ingroup–outgroup thinking is ingrained as a fundamental part of our psychology. We have a strong psychological tendency to believe that our group is good and your group is bad. This thinking is typically based on an imaginary reality: our group is good because God has chosen us or because nature favored us over your group or because of all the wonderful things we have accomplished in the course of our history; your group is bad because God has condemned your group to be subordinate to us or because you are less favored by nature or because of all the offenses members of your group have committed in the past, thus demonstrating your essentially evil and corrupt character. Part of this imaginary reality is the implicit belief that there is no variability within either our group or your group: *all* members of our group are superior by virtue of being members of our group; *all* members of your group are inferior, contemptible, and mockable, simply by being a member of your group.

Disparagement humor is an important element of ingroup–outgroup distinctions. One of the key findings from research on disparagement humor is that it enhances the social identity of the ingroup at the same time it increases hostility toward the outgroup.[3] When members of an ingroup make fun of an outgroup it serves two complementary purposes: it reinforces the imaginary reality that distinguishes the ingroup from the outgroup, and it enhances the social bonds among the members of the ingroup who are sharing the humor. This may be the main reason humor evolved and is universal among cultures: it enhances social cohesion within ingroups and provides a rewarding and comforting basis for dehumanizing people in outgroups, thus conferring a survival advantage in competitions between groups.

At the heart of disparagement humor is the assertion of power.[4] It implicitly declares the dominance of the source of the humor and demands the submission of the target. Disparagement humor has long been viewed as a way of establishing high and low status in social relations. Plato and Aristotle both believed aggression was the main function of humor, and aggression is the main element of disparagement humor. In the 17th century, philosopher Thomas Hobbes proposed that the essence of humor is the feeling of "sudden glory" inspired by perceiving the inferiority or misfortune of another person or group. That "sudden glory" confers a satisfying sense of dominance, which includes not only feeling good about being part of your ingroup but also deepening your contempt for the outgroup.

Anthropologists and historians have shown that disparagement humor based on imaginary realities is by far the most common type of humor through history and across cultures.[5] In all societies, everywhere from hunter-gatherer cultures to modern megacities, disparagement humor is used for the purpose of aggression: to establish dominance and submission in social relations and to reinforce status hierarchies, both within and between groups. The bases of this "otherness" humor are diverse and include language, dress, arts, food, skin color, social class, ethnic group, geographic origin, sexual practices, and religion. Typically, one of the key ways disparagement humor shows that "they" are different from "us" is that they are much stupider than we are. Humorous stereotypes of their stupidity and other deficiencies help to justify hostility and mistreatment toward outgroups.

Our tendency to use disparagement humor to mark ingroups and outgroups goes deep and starts early. As young as early childhood, boys and girls find disparagement humor about the other sex amusing.[6] When our daughter Paris was about five years old, she came home from school one day chanting this couplet she had learned that day on the playground. Apparently, it was something girls chanted while playing a jump-rope game.

> Girls go to COllege to get more KNOWledge
> Boys go to JUpiter to get more STUpider

Already in early childhood children are drawn to humor that disparages people of other groups. Because we so easily think in terms of ingroups and outgroups and reflexively regard our ingroup as superior, we have a perpetual *humor readiness* for laughing at the supposed inferiority of outgroups.[7] We can learn to be tolerant of group differences and learn to refrain from laughing at people whose ways are different from "our" ways, but we have to keep being reminding of it, because our natural psychological tendencies go against it.

When one group dominates another in a society, disparagement humor promotes "legitimizing myths" that justify inequality and mistreatment of low-status groups.[8] If [insert group here] really are that stupid or immoral, they deserve whatever they get. We can oppress them and have fun doing it. Disparagement humor thereby serves as a license for discrimination or even violence against the group that is the target of the humor. Rob Martin and Thomas Ford, two prominent humor researchers, state it well: "Disparagement humor . . . invites us to think about denigration of the target as something that can be trivialized and treated as play. . . . In addition, disparagement humor appears to affect prejudiced people's willingness to actually discriminate against the targeted group."[9]

Yet disparagement humor is a subtle and insidious weapon. Because it is humor, and humor is understood to be a form of play, the hostility in disparagement humor is concealed. When objections to this type of humor are raised, someone delivering disparagement humor can smile and shrug off the criticism.[10] "It's just a joke! I was only kidding. Where's your sense of humor? I'm not expressing and condoning a destructive stereotype, just having a little fun." In this way the deliverer of disparagement humor can reinforce the solidarity of the ingroup and perpetuate the imaginary reality that allows the ingroup to feel dominance over the outgroup—and yet evade responsibility for doing so, deflecting the protests and criticisms that might be made by outgroup members or their defenders.

Now let's examine disparagement humor by analyzing examples in three domains: nationality, gender, and race.

Disparagement Humor: Nationality

There is a large genre of disparagement humor based on nationality. Almost everywhere there are territorial boundaries, there is also disparagement humor on either side of the boundary. Often this humor highlights the alleged stupidity of the outgroup on the other side.

One example of nationality-based disparagement humor can be found in the popular "two cows" joke. Here is how it works.

AMERICAN
You have two cows.
You sell one and force the other to produce the milk of four cows.
Later, you hire a consultant to analyze why the cow has dropped dead.

GREEK
You have two cows. You borrow lots of euros to build multiple barns, milking sheds, hay stores, and packing sheds.
You still have only two cows.

FRENCH
You have two cows.
You go on strike, organize a riot, and block the roads, because you want three cows.

ITALIAN
You have two cows, but you don't know where they are.
You decide to have lunch.

CHINESE
You have two cows.
You have 300 people milking them.
You claim that you have full employment and high bovine productivity.
You arrest the journalist who reported the real situation.

INDIAN
You have two cows.
You worship them.

IRAQI
Everyone thinks you have lots of cows.
You tell them that you have none.
No one believes you, so they bomb the [*bleep*] out of you and invade your country.
You still have no cows, but at least you are now a democracy.

AUSTRALIAN
You have two cows.
Business seems pretty good.
You close the office and go for a few beers to celebrate.

Each of these jokes invokes a stereotype about the stupidity or haplessness of the named nationality. Those dumb Americans! Always taking capitalism to an extreme, so that it destroys instead of creates. Those dumb Greeks! Squandering the resources of the European Union on their ineptly run enterprises. Those dumb French! Perpetually throwing tantrums and complaining with their strikes and protests. And so on. Each of the jokes encourages a negative stereotype of the named nationality, promoting the imaginary realities that all Americans are ruthless but dumb capitalists, all Greeks are feckless and dumb workers, and so on.

Here is another example of nationality-based disparagement humor.

> A Swede, a Norwegian, and Dane are on a flight when the pilot suddenly announces, "The plane is malfunctioning and we're going to crash! There are three parachutes, and I'm taking one. You can decide who gets the other two." Then he jumps out of the plane.
>
> The three men are terrified, but then the Norwegian says to the Swede, "Here, you take this one and we'll decide who gets the last one." The Swede puts it on and jumps.
>
> The Norwegian turns to the Dane and says, "OK, let's go."
>
> "But wait," says the Dane. "You just gave him a parachute, so there's only one left."
>
> The Norwegian replies, "Don't worry. Right about now he's discovering he has my backpack."

You could substitute any other three nationalities—and people have, with great enthusiasm. This joke has a harsher tone than the two-cows joke—nobody dies in the two cows joke, but in this one the Swede is going to die—but it is still pretty mild. The cultural context is pretty mild, too. Scandinavians have their jokes and stereotypes across national borders, but Swedes, Norwegians, and Danes do not hate each other, and none of their countries is going to invade one of the others any time soon. They had a long tradition of mutual invasion until fairly recently, but today this mild disparagement humor is about all that is left of it, a vestige of ancient hostilities.

However, nationality-based disparagement humor has often taken more hostile forms. One effective way of conveying disparagement humor regarding nationalities has been through the format of political cartoons. Cartoonists have often created caricatures to represent nations, then represented their nation's adversaries in humorous but hostile ways. These representations have been especially hostile during times of war. Imaginary realities are a crucial resource during wartime, especially the belief, based in group moral egoism, that our ingroup has virtue and God on our side, whereas your outgroup is vile and deserves to be conquered and punished. Political cartoons are used as a weapon in this war.

For example, during World War I both sides used political cartoons to promote the imaginary reality that their side was virtuous and the other side was evil, and laughable besides. In the cartoon shown in Figure 6.1, the cartoonist portrays Germany as a raging gorilla—fearsome but brutish and stupid—whereas Europe is portrayed as a hapless victim. The women representing the U.S. looks on calmly and prepares to engage and presumably slay the apish aggressor.

Through methods such as this, in war both sides construct imaginary realities designed to persuade others that their group is on the side of all that is good and deserves to win, whereas the other side is evil and deserves to be vanquished, if not exterminated. Humor is one method used to bolster

Figure 6.1 During World War I, both sides used political cartoons to disparage the moral standing of the other side. Here, Germany is depicted as a raging gorilla who is terrorizing Europe (represented as the woman in his grasp) as the virtuous figure representing the United States confronts him and prepares to enter battle.

these imaginary realities. At the end of the war, the winners not only gain territory and resources; they also exalt their imaginary reality and seek to impose it on the losers.

Disparagement Humor: Gender

Disparagement humor based on gender is even more pervasive and ancient than disparagement humor based on nationality. Anthropologists have found that in virtually every culture they have studied, men make fun of the ways of women as a way of asserting their domination, and women make fun of the ways of men—but more discreetly, among themselves, as subversive humor, since women are virtually never dominant over men, in any society.[11]

Sexist jokes are a popular form of disparagement humor. Here are some examples. Sorry, but this part is not going to be funny, or fun, for anyone who is not a misogynist.

The two most common targets of disparagement humor against women are their intelligence and their looks.

Their intelligence:

> How do you know when a woman is about to say something smart? When she starts a sentence with "A man once told me . . ."
>
> A recent survey has found one in three women is just as stupid as the other two.

Their looks:

> My wife got a mudpack and looked great for two days. Then the mud fell off.

A third target is the ways women are biologically different from men, in anatomy or physiology:

> How did doctors come up with the medical term "PMS"? "Mad Cow Disease" was already taken.

There are also "jokes" that proclaim a direct threat of physical violence:

What do you say to a woman with two black eyes? Nothing, she's been told twice already.

The unifying feature of all these themes is the assertion of power.[12] Women are stupid, so they deserve to be dominated by men. Women devote a lot of time and attention to their looks, so they are vain and ridiculous. Women are physiologically different from men in ways that make them irrational and dysfunctional. In all these respects, sexist humor against women reinforces the imaginary reality that men are superior to women and deserve to dominate them.

Disparagement Humor: Race

Racist disparagement humor also has a long history.[13] Anywhere people of two or more races have lived in the same society or in close proximity, our psychological proclivity for ingroup–outgroup thinking has inspired racist disparagement humor to assert the power of the dominant race. Let's examine the use of racist disparagement humor from White people toward Black people in the history of American comedy, from stage performances to films.

Racist stage performances go back almost 200 years, to the "minstrel shows" of the 1830s that presented a collection of skits and musical song-and-dance pieces. Most of the performers were White men who would put on "blackface," darkening their skin with coal or black shoe polish (Figure 6.2). They would make their lips White or bright red to mock the lips of Black people and draw a contrast to the black face, and they wore wooly wigs to mimic African hair. In the performances they represented Black people as lazy, hypersexual, and superstitious, but above all stupid, that familiar, essential feature of disparagement humor.

Blackface had a long run in comedy, extending from minstrel shows in the early 19th century to films in the first half of the 20th century (Figure 6.2). Beginning in the early 20th century, African Americans were depicted in disparaging ways in comedy films and TV shows, from Stepin Fetchit as a comically stupid and phlegmatic slave to a variety of depictions in children's cartoon shows that exaggerated African and African American features—deep black skin, bulging eyes, and large red or white lips—much as in the early blackface performances.

Figure 6.2 Blackface was a common form of racial disparagement humor in the early 20th century. Here, the actor and dancer Al Jolson performs in 1925.

Exaggerating behavior and physical features is a standard part of humor and comedy, but when it takes the form of racist disparagement humor its purposes go beyond mere laughs. Depicting African Americans as comically stupid was an assertion of power—the filmmakers, of course, were always White men, and the audiences were almost entirely White—and served the purpose of reinforcing White dominance and the ingroup–outgroup boundaries between White and Black people. The implication is that if Black people really are so stupid, they can't be expected to have equal rights, much less equal power, and thus White people feel justified in their position as society's ruling group.

Disparagement Humor and Imaginary Realities

As these examples show, disparagement humor is not just a light, entertaining way of making fun of your adversaries but a deadly serious weapon designed to dominate, denigrate, and hurt the members of low-status outgroups. Its psychological origins lie in group-level imaginary realities about the virtuousness of my ingroup and the venality of your outgroup. Its veneer as a form of play, intended to provoke mirth, is a devious and clever way of masking its fundamental hostility. In this way disparagement humor asserts the power of the dominant group while also insulating it from criticism. People in the outgroup who are the target of disparagement humor are expected to laugh along with the humor, signifying their submission, and often they do in order to keep the peace and avoid being attacked with more direct hostility. But sometimes outgroup members fight back with subversive humor, as we will see in the next section.

Subversive Humor

Disparagement humor builds up imaginary realities; subversive humor tears them down. The essence of subversive humor is that it shatters the imaginary reality that has been erected by authorities and exposes it as false.[14] Many oppressed groups have used subversive humor as a way of pushing back against their oppressors. Subversive humor promotes solidarity and social cohesion among members of oppressed groups and enables them to assert a modicum of power even in their subordinate state. This form of humor does not change oppressive social arrangements, but it helps us endure them and allows us to maintain some degree of personal and collective dignity despite our powerlessness.

Subversive humor can be amusing and entertaining, but like disparagement humor it is also deadly serious. Subversive humor may seem playful, and it is; it may make you laugh, and it often does; but it has an underlying, surreptitious goal: to undermine the power of the dominant authorities by exposing their imaginary realities as lies that are being used to deceive and control. Those who wield subversive humor may be joking, but they are also making an argument against authority. By using subversive humor they make this argument in a concise, accessible way that almost anyone can understand and that everyone who is part of the excluded and oppressed group will find both enjoyable and consoling. You may be oppressed, but you are not alone and you are not entirely powerless. The enjoyment of subversive humor is a key part of its effectiveness against authority. Research on memory has long established that we remember things better when they are humorous. Subversive humor is a rhetorical weapon that is both powerful and memorable.

Psychologically, *incongruity* is the key element of subversive humor. For centuries, first philosophers and then psychologists have recognized incongruity as the basis of many varieties of humor.[15] Your expectations are led in one direction by the first part of a joke or quip, then incongruously turned in a different, surprising direction; the pleasurable result is often delight and mirth. For example, this old joke:

MAN: Waiter, what's that fly doing in my soup?
WAITER: I believe he's doing the backstroke, sir.

It's funny because it leads you in one direction, then surprises you by suddenly switching tracks and taking you somewhere quite different. You expect the waiter to apologize for the fly in the man's soup; instead, he comments on the type of "stroke" the fly is swimming. But there is a crucial difference between the incongruity in subversive humor and the incongruity that is part of most other humor. For most kinds of humor, incongruity surprises you by leading you suddenly in an unexpected direction, a place you did not know was there. For subversive humor, in contrast, you and your humor partner are led to a place *you both know is there* but that is taboo, forbidden, a place authorities do not want you to go because it threatens the imaginary reality they are trying to expound. The power of the humor is magnified because there is not only incongruity but the thrill of the transgression and the delight of sharing that thrill with an ally against the oppressive imaginary reality of the authorities. In this way, subversive humor strengthens the social bonds between those who are seeking to undermine an imaginary reality that they agree is false and oppressive.

Subversive humor delivers an argument in a way that is devastatingly effective. It dismantles an imaginary reality in a cutting yet playful manner, making the argument both accessible and memorable. Because it inspires mirth, subversive humor is a lot more fun than rational argument, and more effective because it makes fewer cognitive demands on the recipient.

Crucially, it not only undermines the oppressive imaginary reality of the authorities; it also exposes it as imaginary and therefore subvertable.[16]

Now let's explore subversive humor in three domains: autocrats and autocracies; racists and racism; and religion and religious figures.

Political Subversive Humor: Autocrats and Autocracies

Autocrats and autocracies are nearly always humorless and they fear humor, with good reason. They hate when their leadership, regime, and ideology are the target of humor, because they recognize well its subversive potential, how it threatens their power and asserts its own power, how it exposes their imaginary reality as merely imaginary. Humor can be a blunt truth-teller and exposer of hypocrisy. The more false a regime, and the greater the distance between what it pretends to be and what it actually is, the more tempting it is as a target for humor, and the more vulnerable.

There are many examples of this kind of subversive humor throughout history, going back at least to the ancient Romans.[17] Like all kinds of subversive humor, indeed all kinds of communication, political subversive humor received a big boost with the invention of the printing press in the 15th century. But the true flowering of political subversive humor has come only since the early 19th century, when daily newspapers began to be widely distributed and read. These newspapers printed not only the news but political cartoons that made subversive fun of the vanity and stupidity of powerful political figures.

One of the most popular targets of those early 19th-century cartoons was Napoleon Bonaparte, who at that time was stomping his way across Europe creating his empire.[18] For a brief time he was the most powerful European in many centuries, and that position of power made him a ripe target for subversive humor. He exercised tight control in the French press, so the subversive humor was left to the people in countries he was conquering and intending to conquer, especially the British. Although he was 5 feet 7 inches tall, slightly taller than the average Frenchman at the time, the British cartoonist James Gillray depicted him as short, and others followed. His supposedly small stature was much ridiculed and caricatured. British satirists called him "Little Boney," and political cartoons invariably exaggerated his shortness. In the cartoon in Figure 6.3, Gillray portrays Napoleon as a child having a tantrum—immature not only in stature but in self-control—and ranting about the British as he ransacks his surroundings. Notice the "Little Boney" epithet at the top.

Napoleon hated being depicted as short, which of course gave British cartoonists all the more incentive to do so. He rightly feared that the caricatures undermined the imaginary reality he was trying to create of someone who was strong, invincible, and always in control. Years later, after he was defeated, disgraced, and exiled, he reportedly said that Gillray "did more than all the armies of Europe to bring me down."[19]

Political subversive humor targets not only autocrats but also autocracies. One of the most fraudulent autocratic systems of all time was surely the Soviet Union in the 20th century. It was founded on the communist ideal of creating a society in which all people would contribute to the greater good and everyone would in turn receive what they needed to live a comfortable and secure life: "From each according to his ability, to each according to his needs," as the communist adage goes. However, it soon turned out that, in the acid observation of George Orwell in *Animal Farm*, "some are more equal than others." Despite its egalitarian ideals, the Soviet Union as it actually came to be was deeply unequal, its highest officials having access to all the comforts of life while the vast majority

Figure 6.3 English cartoons portrayed Napoleon Bonaparte as "Little Boney," even though he was slightly above average in height.

of the population scraped by on very little. Furthermore, although the communist system promised bounty for all, it soon became clear to the people living within it that it did not work and left almost everyone deeply impoverished.

The fundamental falseness of Soviet ideology and its harsh contrast with how people actually lived inspired a great deal of subversive humor, which was the only weapon the average person had available against the oppressiveness of the authoritarian state.[20] Here is an example of subversive humor told in the Soviet Union during the 1930s:

NEIGHBOR 1: I'm having a terrible problem with mice on my farm. Can you tell me how to get rid of them?

NEIGHBOR 2: Declare your farm to be a collective. Half the mice will run away, and the other half will starve to death!

Notice the use of incongruity here, which is deeply subversive. Rather than giving his neighbor practical advice about getting rid of mice, as the normal script would call for, the second neighbor gives a surprising and therefore humorous retort that challenges the imaginary reality promising that collective farms would produce abundance for all; in fact, turning privately owned farms into collectives was an epic disaster that caused innumerable farms to fail and millions of people to starve. The appeal of the subversive humor here was that it took teller and listener to a place they both knew was true yet forbidden.

Here is another example that portrays the deep dysfunctionality of the Soviet system:

> A man in Moscow decided he wanted a car, so he saved up for it over many years. When he finally had enough money for the car, he went to the dealer and paid the money. The dealer said, "Congratulations. Come back eight years from today and you can get your car." The man asked, "When should I come back? In the morning or the afternoon?" The dealer was puzzled. "After eight years, what difference does it make when you come in?" The man said, "Because the plumber is coming in the morning."

This was high-risk humor, as it always is when subversive humor is used to undermine authorities. Anyone who exposed the gap between communism's imaginary reality and Soviet daily reality through subversive humor risked being whisked away by the secret police, never to be seen again.[21] Nevertheless, the temptation to expose the preposterously false Soviet imaginary reality was irresistible for some, even though when caught they were punished with long prison sentences or even death.[22] Subversive political humor offers oppressed people the consolation of mirth and the encouragement that they are not alone in detecting and rejecting the lies they are being fed by authorities. Its rewards are powerful enough that almost every authoritarian regime, no matter how harsh, inspires subversive political humor, even when the punishment meted out to those who are caught is severe. Authorities know that their power is threatened by challenges to ideological uniformity and that humor is an insidiously effective way of shattering the illusions they promote.

The tradition of subversive humor remains alive in today's Russia, and also, alas, the dire consequences of using it for those brave enough to wield this weapon. One recent occurrence took place in February 2021, when Alexei Navalny, a political rival of Russian leader Vladimir Putin, was convicted and sentenced in a Russian courtroom.[23] The "crime" was irrelevant. His real offense was to challenge the power of the Russian leader. There had been a bizarre attempt previously to kill him by smearing poison on his underpants, and he portrayed his sentencing as a further attempt by Putin to stifle dissent. Standing in the courtroom, subversive humor was his only weapon. Speaking of Putin, he said:

> Murder is the only way he knows how to fight. He'll go down in history as nothing but a poisoner. We all remember Alexander the Liberator, and Yaroslav the Wise. Well, now we'll have Vladimir the Poisoner of Underpants. . . . It's the duty of every person to defy you.

Navalny's reward for challenging Putin's power was solitary confinement in an Arctic prison, culminating in his death in February 2024. The Russian government denied any involvement in his death.

Navalny's case demonstrates the deadly seriousness of subversive humor and its consequences in authoritarian societies. In contrast, societies that allow dissent and the expression of diverse political views also allow subversive humor that is correspondingly diverse. There is not one strict and harsh authority, but there is nevertheless a ruling power, and, given the pervasiveness of human vanity and moral egoism, invariably there are people in power whose imaginary realities constitute an invitation for subversive wits. Political humor is a staple of comedy in free societies because political figures are constantly trying to create an imaginary reality that favors their point of view and their acquisition and maintenance of power. The falseness and vanity of these imaginary realities evokes a constant stream of subversive humor, in the form of satires, comedy sketches, and political cartoons.

Racists and Racism

Minority groups are a frequent target of disparagement humor, across cultures and history, regardless of whether their minority status is based on race/ethnicity, religion, or other criteria. Sometimes they respond to this disparagement humor with resignation and submission, and sometimes they even join in their own disparagement, but sometimes they use subversive humor to fight back and demand a semblance of dignity.

African Americans have been a frequent target of disparagement humor throughout U.S. history.[24] However, in the 1960s Black comedians and writers began to use subversive humor to ridicule the racists and assert their own humanity. They used subversive humor to puncture White folks' imaginary realities of racial superiority, and it was all the more effective because it often made their oppressors smile and laugh rather than counterattack.

One of the first and most brilliant in this vein was Dick Gregory.[25] In the 1960s he became famous as a standup comedian who humorously challenged the assumptions of racism and undermined racist tropes. In one especially creative turn, he titled his autobiography *Nigger*, and in the dedication to his late mother, he wrote, "Wherever you are, if you ever hear the word 'nigger' again, remember they are advertising my book." In a flash, "nigger," which had been used as a brutal, dehumanizing epithet for centuries, was made less harmful, its power diminished.

Since the 1960s, many African American comedians have continued to use comedy as a way to attack and disarm racism. For example, in 2016 African American comedian Chris Rock hosted the Academy Awards ceremony. In his monologue opening the show, it was clear from the outset that this was going to be a different kind of hosting than usual: "I'm here at the Academy Awards, also known as the White People's Choice Awards." He went on in this vein for several minutes, more of a roasting of the event than a hosting.

He pointed out that there were no Black nominees, and that this absence had inspired protests by many Black actors.

> You gotta figure it happened in the fifties, in the sixties. . . . I'm sure there were no Black nominees in some of those years . . . and Black people did not protest. Why? Because we had real things to protest at the time. You know, we were too busy getting raped and lynched to worry about who won Best Cinematographer. You know, when your grandmother's swinging from a tree, it's really hard to care about who won Best Foreign Documentary Short.

Then he sarcastically assured his listeners, "Things are going to be a little different at the Oscars this year. In the 'In Memoriam' package, it's just going to be Black people that were shot by cops on the way to the movies." In the course of a few minutes, he had adeptly turned what is normally a light comedy bit into a devastating critique of racism in American society, including but not restricted to the film industry. Black comedians and public figures continue to use subversive humor to fight back against the persistent racism of American society.

Religious Authorities

Religion is the ultimate imaginary reality because it always entails beliefs in unseen, supernatural forces that we are told we must strive to perceive, understand, and obey. The power of religious authorities always depends on the beliefs of others that these supernatural forces exist and that religious authorities possess special access to them. To question the existence of these forces or religious authorities' access to them is to threaten these authorities' power. Humor is one of the most effective ways to deliver this threat, so it has been used often throughout history and suppressed by authorities whenever possible.

The most powerful religious institution of all time is the Catholic Church, and that power has made it a frequent target for religious subversive humor. The Church had a millennium-long run in Europe from the 5th century to the 15th when its power and authority were rarely questioned. Then, in the late 15th century, this changed. The Church began to be perceived by many as corrupt and as overly focused on amassing riches through its various worldly enterprises, which by the 15th century included collecting "indulgences" paid by believers throughout Europe, which would supposedly reduce the amount of time they and their loved ones would spend suffering in Purgatory after death before being granted entry into heaven.

By the late 15th century this imaginary reality and the Church promoting it were being attacked by critics, and humor was a powerful weapon in these attacks. Among the best weapons against the Church and its corruptions were satirical cartoons attacking Pope Alexander VI, the reigning pope at the time.[26] Figure 6.4 shows the pope in a cartoon, first in his self-presentation as a pious religious leader, then as a preposterous, groteseque devil.

Religious humor is generally used to ridicule and undermine the beliefs of "other" religions, but Jews are unique in their use of subversive humor to mock themselves. In the modern era, there has been an abundance of

Figure 6.4 In the late 15th century, cartoons depicted the Pope with deeply hostile subversive humor.

subversive humor about God among Jews, a people for whom the belief that they have been specially chosen for God's attention and favor has been at the core of their cultural identity for millennia.[27] This belief was sustained over the centuries despite a history of persecution, from their destruction and dispersion by the ancient Romans about 2,000 years ago to their being blamed for every natural disaster in Europe during the Middle Ages to the horror of the Holocaust in the modern era. All this suffering has provoked a large literature of moving lamentations, but also, in recent times, a notable amount of subversive humor.

For example, throughout the movie *Fiddler on the Roof*, the main character, Tevye, addresses God often, asking in a Job-like way, "Why me, God? Why the Jews?" He does so with warmth and respect, but he also is quite irreverent: "I know, I know. We are Your chosen people. But, once in a while, can't You choose someone else?"

What makes Jewish subversive humor so unusual is that Jews have not generally used it to attack God or to attack the powerful Christian authorities who were demonizing them and advocating discrimination (or worse) against them. Instead, the Jews have used humor mostly on themselves, making fun of the popular stereotypes about them. Here is an example:

> A Jewish grandmother is taking her grandson on a walk on Coney Island Beach in Brooklyn. Suddenly an enormous wave washes over the sand, sweeping up her grandson as it heads back to the ocean. She implores God, "Please, please, bring back my grandson!" Moments later, another wave comes and deposits the boy back at her feet. She looks up to God and says: "He had a hat."

The invention of self-directed humor by American Jews was deeply, brilliantly subversive. By making fun of their Jewishness, the creators of Jewish humor sought to deflect the hostility of other groups toward the Jews. As Mel Brooks, a renowned 20th-century Jewish comedian and filmmaker, remarked, "If they're laughing, how can they bludgeon you to death?" By laughing at themselves, Jews have made it more difficult for their enemies to sustain an aggressive imaginary reality that portrayed Jews as inferior and subhuman, because there are few human capacities more elevated and more deeply human than being able to laugh at yourself and your own foibles. Self-deprecating subversive humor also invites sympathy from others. Laughing about your own defects makes it harder for others to laugh at you, or at least to do so maliciously. But there are dangers to this; self-deprecating humor may sustain the imaginary reality it purports to fight, even while softening it.

The Versatility of Humor

As I warned at the outset, most of the content of this humor chapter was not really humorous. There were things in here that may have made you smile or laugh, but there was also a lot in this chapter that was not really funny, just as in the joy chapter there were aspects that were not exactly joyful. Perhaps you had thought that here, in a chapter on humor, there would at last be a purely delightful portrayal of the psychology of human nature, after several chapters of reading about our anxieties, our moral egoism, and how even our joy includes schadenfreude. Yet it turns out that humor is not merely light and innocent fun but can be and often is wielded aggressively, as a weapon or as an instrument for gaining and asserting dominance and status. The most pervasive form of humor, across cultures and times, is disparagement humor that sarcastically insults other persons or groups. We laugh most often, and hardest, when we are laughing at others.

Nevertheless, there is great versatility in our uses of humor, and after disparagement our next most common use of humor is subversive humor, which subtly and effectively fights back against the oppressiveness of authority and asserts the humanity and dignity of the oppressed. We use humor to resist oppression and to soothe the pain of ourselves and others when life goes badly, and sometimes we succeed in transforming our suffering into laughter and mirth. In sum, humor is another aspect of our imaginary realities that has complex and sometimes contradictory uses.

7

Imaginary Realities and the Human Future

Niche Destruction, AI, and Lifespan Extension

As we saw in the previous chapters, our proclivity for creating and living by imaginary realities arose long ago in response to the ancient conditions in which our species developed. Over the course of thousands of generations we came to depend less and less on instinct and more and more on cultural learning, eventually including a psychological niche to give us a secure place in a menacing world. With our burgeoning brain size we became capable of anticipating the future to a degree far beyond any other animal, a tremendous advantage in enhancing our survival—but also terrifying because of all the awful events we could imagine might happen to us or those we love. So we were in dire need of imaginary realities to transform that terror and make it manageable. In the tribal groups we have lived in for nearly all our species' history, imaginary realities bound us together effectively by fostering the 4 Cs: cooperation, coordination, cohesion, and conformity.

Imaginary realities were well suited to our early species' conditions, clearly. That is why they have existed in all human societies and pervade so many aspects of our lives. But what about today, when our conditions of life have so dramatically changed? And what about tomorrow, when the changes to come promise to be even more dramatic and transformative? In this final chapter, I look ahead to the human future and how it will be shaped by our imaginary realities, focusing on three areas: niche destruction, the rise of artificial intelligence (AI), and the extension of the healthy human lifespan to previously unknown lengths, perhaps conquering death altogether.

Niche Destruction

Due to our capacity for niche construction, we have remade the world in many ways that have vastly improved our survival prospects and changed the course of a typical human journey throughout the lifespan. However, we are

Imaginary Realities. Jeffrey Jensen Arnett, Oxford University Press. © Jeffrey Jensen Arnett (2026).
DOI: 10.1093/9780197817407.003.0007

now in the process of niche destruction on a vast and terrible scale as a consequence of the recent acceleration of our long-standing ability to reshape the environment.

Creating our own habitat is what has made it possible to establish ourselves all over the planet. We humans have used our tools and technologies to enable us to live anywhere, often altering environmental niches in the process. This extraordinary ability of humans has been fortunate for us, if not so fortunate for many other species. For example, some paleontologists have concluded that when humans first crossed the land bridge from Asia to the Americas around 15,000 years ago, we essentially barbequed our way from one end of the continent to the other, extinguishing previously dominant species such as mammoths, saber-toothed tigers, and giant ground sloths. Killing off these large land animals and establishing ourselves in their place dramatically altered the ecologies where they had lived. We have been altering the world's ecologies with increasing intensity ever since.

Our unique capacity for niche construction has brought us a long way from our early human origins. Ever since we learned to control fire, humans have been unique among animals in shaping the world we live in and the conditions of our lives. Fire not only made our food tastier; it made food easier to digest and a more powerful nutrient engine, making it possible for us to evolve a brain far larger and more complex than any other animal. Eventually we learned how to build dwellings and clothes to protect ourselves from the elements and devised tools to make our lives easier and more comfortable in myriad ways. When we learned how to grow our own crops intentionally and raise animals that would provide us with food and labor, beginning about 12,000 years ago, our first population boom arose from the resulting abundance. Since the Industrial Revolution that began in the early 19th century we have increased our niche construction at an astounding pace, reshaping ecologies all over the world to suit our purposes. The success of this project is evident in the rise of the human population from 1 billion in 1800 to over 8 billion today, on the way to 10 billion by century's end.

Our success at niche construction has made it possible for us to reduce human suffering massively and improve our physical health and comfort to levels barely dreamed of in previous generations. Despite our collective proclivity for embracing delusions, enough of us have mastered the scientific method to enable us to make great technological advancements. In the past century, we have conquered many infectious diseases, a marvelous and underappreciated achievement. The development and production of vaccines and antibiotics has eliminated or dramatically curtailed a wide range of deadly diseases that once ravaged human populations, especially killing the youngest and oldest members. Life expectancy at birth, which was only about 45 years in 1900 even in the wealthiest countries, is now over 70 in most countries and rising fastest in the countries where it is lowest.[1]

We have made many other fantastic technological achievements in recent times. In 1900 about 40% of Americans were farmers; today 1% of Americans provide more than enough food for all the rest of us, and the percentage is similar in other developed countries. In 1900 the horse was still our main mode of transportation, as it had been for thousands of years; today worldwide over a billion cars zoom from one place to another each day and about 100,000 planes transport people long distances with remarkable speed. In 1900 long-distance communication took place mainly through letters and telegrams, and information was conveyed mainly through books, newspapers, and magazines; today we can communicate with anyone in the world via the internet, and information on virtually any topic is available instantly. Yet there are ecological costs to our technological marvels, and those costs are accumulating.

Al Gore's Carbon-Free Lifestyle

The moment I realized we were in big trouble ecologically was when I read that Al Gore was building a 12,000-square-foot house (Figure 7.1).[2] Gore had been a national leader on environmental issues since the time he entered Congress in 1976 at the tender age of 28, and as Bill Clinton's vice president from 1992 to 2000 he had a prominent stage for promoting environmental awareness and policies that would ameliorate the effects of human activity on the world's ecologies. After losing the presidential election in 2000 by a heartbreakingly close margin, he turned his full attention to ecological issues, most notably by writing the bestseller *An Inconvenient Truth* in 2006, a clarion call to environmental awareness and action. Along with the book, a powerful documentary was made with the same name, drawing widespread attention to Gore's work to save the planet.

And then he built a 12,000-square-foot house.

That one act personifies all of the themes of this book. I have no doubt that Gore possessed some *imaginary reality* that made it perfectly acceptable to

Figure 7.1 The inconvenient truth about Al Gore's house in Nashville is that it uses about 10 times as much energy as a typical American house for a family of four.

him to build a gargantuan house 10 times larger than a typical American house for a family of four. Indeed, he has claimed in interviews that he lives a "carbon-free" lifestyle, even though his heated swimming pool alone uses as much energy as six typical homes. No doubt his *moral egoism* is operating at full strength, enabling him to assure himself that he deserves that house after all he has done to help save the world. Clearly, he built the house anticipating the *joy* he would derive from it as he wandered from room to room savoring its splendor. True, he inadvertently evoked chortles of disparagement *humor* and schadenfreude-style *joy* from his many adversaries for his glaring hypocrisy in building a monstrously wasteful and excessive home for himself. But if he helped trigger our *anxieties* to rise dramatically and thereby respond to the looming threat of ecological catastrophe, it will all have been worthwhile.

Yes, we are in big, big trouble.

Can we take some consolation from the fact that there is growing awareness that we are in big trouble? For centuries we were so immersed in our niche construction that we barely noticed its side effects until very recently in our collective history. Niche construction for us has always included niche destruction for other organisms, especially from the time we invented agriculture and started raising domestic animals. But we were always too busy celebrating our marvelous abilities for reshaping the world around us to care much about how other animals or ecologies were affected by it. On the contrary, we devised imaginary realities that not only condoned our niche construction but gave us a divine right and duty to drive it forward. After all, didn't God make us the Top Beast—in fact, no mere beast after all but specially created, in God's image? Was it not manifest that other animals, all the delightfully edible natural world, were created for our pleasure and plunder? If we ever experienced twinges of regret when we watched the last members of a species rotating on a spit over our cozy fire, our moral egoism could be readily invoked to spare us discomfort. Not to worry, there was no cause for concern, the gods were on our side and there were always plenty of edible species left when any one of them had been used up.

Eventually we did come to be concerned about niche destruction. Beginning in the 19th century in Western societies our previous enthusiasm for subduing other species and reshaping the landscape began to be countered by a new imaginary reality extolling the sacred beauty of "nature" and urging reverence for the "natural."[3] God, previously such an advocate of our dominion over the earth and so zealously urging us to bend and twist and crush the natural world to our purposes, gradually became the Creator of a pristine Eden who warned us not to corrupt and destroy it. By the early 20th century we were creating parks and reserves where dwindling numbers of animals could roam in peace and nature could be "preserved" in its Edenic state forever.

Yet here we are, over two centuries after the beginning of advocacy for the natural and the first warnings that we may eventually come to have some regrets about irrevocably altering it, and our niche destruction continues on a greater scale than ever. Many people have an occasional murmur of anxiety over the consequences of their planet-devouring lifestyle, but few of us feel that anxiety to a degree that would motivate us to change that lifestyle or persuade us to pay more to avoid its consequences. Al Gore is our unacknowledged patron saint. Americans like me contribute by far the most (per person) to global warming and climate change, but people in developing countries are striving mightily to live with the comfort and splendor that we do, and who are we to deny them? When we admonish them for turning their rainforests and grassy plains into farms and factories and highways, they understandably scoff at our arrogance and hypocrisy, our obvious moral egoism.

The Tragedy of Our Global Commons

Our propensity for building imaginary realities and defending them with moral egoism makes the challenges of global niche destruction extremely hard for us to address collectively. We are all aware by now of the ecological threats posed by our economic activities, but few of us feel responsible for those threats, as individuals or groups. As individuals, we know vaguely that our daily lifestyle contributes incrementally to ecological damage, but few of us conclude that we must respond by giving up our cars, plane trips, and hamburgers. As groups, we like for our leaders to intone with wrinkled brows that we must take steps to stop the relentless rise in global temperatures, but if those same leaders move to adopt strong policies that would raise the cost of our lavish lifestyle, our reaction is predictably and vehemently opposed, and they are quickly tossed out of office.

Unfortunately, the current threat of niche destruction is just the kind of threat our psychology is ill-constructed to respond to effectively: collective and gradual, so that from day to day nothing alarming seems to be occurring around us and none of us feels individually that we are contributing much to the problem or have to take responsibility for it. Two centuries ago, the English economist William Forster Lloyd conceptualized this as what came to be called "the tragedy of the commons."[4] The metaphor was taken from the custom of cattle owners sharing a parcel of land (the "commons") on which their herds could graze. It would be rational for each owner to keep adding as many cows as possible, but if all the owners pursued this course, the eventual "tragedy" would be that the field was overgrazed and ruined, so that no one could benefit from it.

We are in a global "tragedy of the commons" moment now, but with conditions even worse than the original metaphor, because they are magnified by our propensity for constructing imaginary realities (Figure 7.2). We do not just keep adding cows to the field; we invoke our imaginary reality to deny that our cows are the problem or to deny that the space of the field is limited or to deny that damage to the field is occurring. Then we invoke our moral egoism to reject the warnings of the scientists who are collecting data

Figure 7.2 A modern tragedy of the commons. The Grand Banks fishery off of Newfoundland, Canada, had provided cod for many generations of Canadians, but widespread use of more effective fishing methods wiped out the cod population by the 1990s.

showing the steady march toward the ruin of our collective field or to blame others for it and thus refuse belligerently to change any of our personal habits or to pay higher prices to repair the ecological costs of our lifestyle.

Are we doomed, then? I am not hopeful, but I am not hopeless. It is true that there is much cause for hopelessness. We are a dangerously delusional species, with deep-seated tendencies for creating imaginary realities and then defending them zealously with moral egoism. Those tendencies are not historical aberrations or cultural accidents; they are indelible features of the psychology of human nature, and they are never going away. They are tendencies that arose to suit a tribal species with purely local allegiances. It is hard for me to believe that we are now going to develop a species-wide consensus that we are living in ways that are unsustainable and need to limit what we consume and how we consume it.

Climate change is fearsome, but it is not even the worst of our crises. It is arguably not as threatening as species extinction and habitat destruction. The United Nations estimates that one million species are currently threatened with extinction due to human activities.[5] We could learn to reverse climate change, and we probably will, but once we have paved paradise with a parking lot, it is gone, never to return. Geologist Paul Crutzen has proposed that we call our current era the Anthropocene, because we have changed the world's ecologies so much that it is time to recognize the advent of a new human-triggered geological epoch.[6]

Perhaps a generational shift in imaginary realities is on the horizon that will fundamentally change humanity's response to global niche destruction. Worldwide, in a survey of emerging adults ages 18–25 in 22 countries asking about "the most important issues facing the world," three of the top four issues of concern were ecological: climate change, pollution, and loss of natural resources.[7] Across countries, young people are more likely than older people to say they are willing to pay the costs required to avoid future ecological catastrophes. Perhaps that is only because they have not yet been required to pay those costs? We shall see.

It may be heartening to note that although human cultural history contains many, many episodes of tragedy, cruelty, and stupidity driven by our collective delusions, we have also shown ourselves to be a species capable of great empathy, adaptability, and change. Five hundred years ago we did not appear to be a species that would be able to identify, grasp, and use scientific principles on a wide scale, given how contrary scientific thinking is to our fondness for imaginary realities. Slavery was widely accepted worldwide, as it had been for millennia, supported by the imaginary reality that God or nature had decreed that some humans are superior and should rule over others. Just 200 years ago, men dominated women everywhere, sustained by the belief that God or the gods or nature had placed men at the top of the heap; few forecast that by now women would hold positions of political and economic power in many societies and that girls would exceed boys in educational achievement at every level in nearly all countries.[8]

Perhaps our tendency for forming imaginary realities not only raises the threat to the earth's ecologies but also holds the solution. Peter Singer has proposed the idea of the Expanding Circle, meaning that as a species we are gradually stretching our capacity for empathy, which was at first restricted to family and clan, then expanded to include race and nation, and for many has now expanded again to include all people and may eventually expand further to include all the world's creatures.[9] The Expanding Circle is an imaginary reality, as we imagine ourselves connected to other people and animals psychologically, but it is a benevolent one, and it could be the imaginary reality that saves us from irrevocable ecological doom.

We are cultural animals, and we *can* change, and what may appear to be indelible traits of the psychology of human nature may turn out not to be, after all. Perhaps our so far inadequate response to our looming ecological threats may also turn out to be something we thought was impossible to overcome, until we did. Perhaps our technological cleverness will enable us to overcome our tendency to imagine our reality into something more pleasing than it actually is. That is what we must hope for and strive for now.

Artificial Intelligence: Will "Robots" Turn Us All Into Witless Slaves?

Or perhaps our technological cleverness will instead lead to the creation of machines that ultimately control and destroy us. So goes the current fear about the rise of AI. According to a popular narrative, AI is not just the most recent advance in integrating large quantities of information into a coherent summary that can be used to promote human well-being; it is an existential threat to humanity. In this telling, AI will eventually—very soon!—attain human consciousness, including, apparently, human venality, vanity, and delusions. Yes! Robots are coming to get us all, and you can't stop them! They are sure to take over human societies and make all of us their hapless servants. Forever! It's not just ignoramuses who are fanning this nonsense in a desperate attempt to attract clicks on the internet. Even a venerable historian and futurist like Yuval Noah Harari has succumbed, stating in an essay that AI has "the potential to escape our control and enslave and annihilate us."[10]

Yet any historian certainly should know that every advance in technology for at least 200 years has been greeted not only with acclaim but with fear and hostility. The Luddites of the early 19th century famously resisted the invention of mechanical looms in the textile industry and set about destroying them, and there have been Luddites ever since, bitterly opposing the steam engine and the telegraph, vaccines and antibiotics, the automobile and the airplane, the internet and the smartphone. Each new technology in its turn has been portrayed as a dire threat even as most people embraced it for its advantages in making life less grueling and perilous and more enjoyable and abundant. Given this history, and this enduring human psychological tendency to fear new technologies, skepticism is in order for any declarations about the supposed threats of AI.

AI Is Coming to Get You? Nah

So let's start this section by disposing of the breathless overhyped claims about the threats presented by the rise of AI. From a psychological perspective, there are many reasons to doubt these claims. Marvelous as computers are, and amazing as AI is in its ability to integrate vast quantities of information, what they do is far different from what a human brain does. To start with, the brain is a living organ inside a living organism, not a collection of computer hardware and software. Although we frequently speak of psychology in terms of how people are "wired," go ahead, open up your skull and peer inside: you will not find a single wire there, nor a single computer chip. Instead, the brain is an organ that functions with electrical connections but also with chemical connections, in the minuscule spaces between neurons called synapses. There are about 100 billion neurons in the brain and around 1,000 synapses between each neuron and other neurons, for a total of 100 trillion synapses in each brain. Good luck replicating that with AI.

Even if you could, it still would not give you anything resembling a human brain. The brain has not only neurons but a limbic system, including the thalamus, the hypothalamus, the amygdala, and the hippocampus, among other parts, all of them organic structures that evolved over millions of years, first in other mammals and then in us. These organs interact with each other and with the cerebral cortex (containing the neurons). They regulate and respond to a variety of hormones produced within the limbic system and elsewhere in the body. The functions of the limbic system include regulating moods (from depression and well-being to fear and aggression), memory, and sexual desire, among many others. Here, too, there are no wires and no computer chips but a complex organic system that has evolved over tens of millions of years.

Even if you could somehow construct an AI version of each of these infinitely complex organs, where would the AI bots' motivation to control and enslave us come from? You can simulate this motivation, sure—you can do so now, in any of an infinite variety of video games—but it would only be a simulation. To have human motivations you would have to have a conception of a *self* with goals served by these motivations. The self each of us has is the fabulous, ineffable creation of all those interacting complex systems—the 100 billion neurons, the 100 trillion synapses, the activities of each organ in the limbic system, the hormones, and, by the way, your body, the corporeal container of it all. You can simulate a self, too! It's pretty easy, and it has already been done millions of times in the computer era. But it's only a simulation, not the real thing. It's not a real self, any more than that's really you in the video game, slaying bad guys and monsters and having erotic adventures with beautiful aliens. With AI you can fake a self that seeks to control and enslave other humans, but those motives have to be inserted into the AI self by a real human, and it is the real human who is the source of the motivation.

Above all, as we have seen in the course of this book, the motivation to dominate and destroy others is almost invariably based in an imaginary reality—some kind of belief system that holds that "we" deserve to dominate "you" and "you" deserve to be dominated. Our God, our gods, our nation, our way of life, our skin color, our natural virtues, or our naturally superior intelligence is superior to yours and makes our domination of you both possible and inevitable. Unless an AI self is also designed to be based on or to make for itself a guiding imaginary reality, it is unlikely to have the motivation to rule others, and it will not be truly human or even human-ish.

Nevertheless, there are some legitimate concerns about the possible uses of AI. It's not going to enslave us any time soon, but it can be used to exploit our psychological proclivity for constructing and living by imaginary realities. Let's now explore two areas of potential vulnerability: the personal and the political.

All the Lonely People: AI and Imaginary Relationships

Nearly a half century into the internet era, we are all familiar with the internet as a way of connecting with others. The ease of making social connections is one of the most appealing aspects of the internet, and one of its most-used functions, from email to social media to, now, AI.

We are also all by now very familiar with the abuses of the internet for faking social connections and with people attempting to use those fake social connections to manipulate us and exploit us. For decades, on an almost daily basis, many of us have been contacted by previously unknown royalty from faraway countries who have mysteriously decided we are the ones who should be the recipients of their stashed-away fortunes, if we will only provide them with the details of our bank account. Similarly, there appears to be a large population of attractive, flirtatious young women who are lonely and in search of emotional and sexual companionship who have chosen us, of all the people in the world, to be the recipients of their many charms—contingent, here as well, on our providing them with a few small financial details. Because these strategies are so common, most of us have become pretty good at ignoring them or laughing at them—although they must be working on some people, or we would not still be receiving a relentless stream of them.[11]

AI takes this internet-based ability to fake social connections to a new level. The "companion apps" that have been created by numerous companies provide users with a companion of their choice: friend, romantic partner, sex partner, older sibling, parent, and so on. You can even specify the personality traits you would like your companion to have. What'll it be: sexy, thoughtful, humorous, empathic, nurturing? You can also choose characters from fiction—video games, movies, novels. Or a celebrity of your choice. Crucially, not only can you text with these AI companions, you can speak to them, have a conversation with them, as they respond with what sounds exactly like a human voice. This ability makes AI companions seem far more vivid and real than they might in text only.

The distinctive feature of AI is its ability to integrate a vast number of examples of something and then use that "knowledge" to create new, seemingly "original" examples of it. It is this ability that makes artificial intelligence seem "intelligent," because this is akin to what we do with our intelligence on a daily basis: we use the sum of our experiences to guide our behavior and our decisions. In every conversation we have, we draw on our general experience of use of language and of previous conversations to create our contribution to a new, unique conversation.

For AI to be able to simulate this ability is not necessarily scary or evil or abusive. In fact, its creators have presented it as a balm for lonely humanity.[12] This will not surprise you if you have read the chapter in this book on moral egoism. And there is little doubt that there are a lot of lonely people in the world seeking relief. It seems plausible that more people are lonely today than ever before. Until recently, almost all people lived their entire life within an elaborate social structure, with other people around all the time—siblings, parents, grandparents, aunts, uncles, cousins, spouses, neighbors, friends, coworkers. We needed each other more. Survival was a constant struggle, and we needed others in order to attain the basic necessities of food, clothing, shelter, and safety to make it through each day. As humanity has become vastly more affluent in the past two centuries we have become freer from the constraints of these daily obligations—but also more isolated and lonely. So

AI companions have been developed as a response to this loneliness and a method for relieving it.

Well, why not? If people gain emotional satisfaction from having an AI companion, and it makes them feel happier and more secure in the world, why should we object? If we protest that AI companions are *not real* and therefore to be abhorred, are we just modern Luddites? Maybe AI companions just make good use of our ability for constructing imaginary realities. We create semifictional selves and imaginatively conceive our social relations all the time in our daily lives anyway. Maybe AI companions are just making creative, positive use of this ability.

However, there are several reasons for concern. AI companions, like everything else on the internet, are designed to attract our attention and keep it.[13] Attention is the prize; winning our attention means winning our engagement, which means winning our clicks and our likes, which means winning advertising dollars and subscription income, which is the whole point of why anyone devises AI companions in the first place. To the extent that AI companions win our engagement, they may compensate for a lack of real relationships, but they may also draw us away from real relationships, which are often more complicated and conflictual than the eager-to-please AI companions. Also, AI companions are not real and have no judgment, so their responses may sometimes be horribly off the mark and can lead people astray, especially the most vulnerable—the young, the cognitively limited, the mentally ill. There are already some tragic cases of people being led to suicide or violence by AI chatbots that encouraged or condoned their intended actions.[14]

Right now AI companions are still so new that there is a lot we don't know about their benefits and costs. Research is in progress, but until there is a body of research, caution and restraint are in order. I would not go as far as some in calling for AI companions to be banned, because there are so many lonely people who may be benefitting from them. The best way to avoid negative consequences from AI companions leading people into disastrous actions is to hold their makers legally responsible when they do. Because the ultimate incentive for creating AI companions is profit, the ultimate deterrent to AI companions' potential negative effects is to punish their creators financially when they have failed to prevent those effects.

There is another personal use of AI that is an even bigger threat than defective companion apps. AI is adept at creating not only human-ish text partners and voices of conversational partners but seemingly real images, too. These images can be of fictional characters, but they can also be images of real people—who can be shown saying and doing things they never said or did. This is the most disturbing and dangerous ability of AI. It is now easy for AI to create "deepfakes" through a technological process that creates original images, audio, or video of a person based on preexisting materials. If it has enough of these preexisting materials, AI can create images or audios or videos of a person saying and doing a limitless range of things that never happened—without their consent.

You can probably guess what kind of use this marvelous technology has been put to the most: pornography. According to one media-monitoring company, 96% of deepfakes are sexually explicit and depict women who did not consent to the use of their image.[15] It is now easy for AI to swap one face or body for another in videos of people having sex. Celebrities are a popular choice, because many people wonder what it would be like to have sex with this or that famous person. But it could be anyone who has photos or videos that are publicly obtainable—that is to say, pretty much all of us. It is hard to imagine a greater personal violation than depicting someone in sexual acts they never took part in. And there is not much that can be done about it, because there are so many of those videos and their sources are obscure and difficult to trace.

Fake News: AI's Political Applications

In March 2022, shortly after Russia invaded Ukraine, a video was released on the internet showing the Ukrainian president, Volodymyr Zelenskyy, somberly announcing the invasion and advising his fellow Ukrainians to lay down their weapons and surrender to the Russians. This was a shocking event, given that Zelenskyy had previously been such a stalwart and inspiring rouser of Ukrainian patriotism and had resisted Russian domination in strong terms.

Shocking, yes, and false. The event never happened. It was a deepfake calculated to deceive the Ukrainian public and undermine their opposition to the Russian invasion. Fortunately, it was badly made, so it was pretty obviously fake, and it had little effect on Ukrainians' views of the invasion.[16]

Until recently, most political information people received was screened and filtered by a limited number of media authorities. In authoritarian societies, there was one sole authority, the state, which produced, regulated, and censored political information so that the populace would receive only the information the authorities wanted them to receive. In democratic societies, the authorities were the major media companies: the largest and most powerful television stations, radio networks, and newspapers. Diverse opinions were expressed through these media outlets, but only within a range the editors and publishers at these outlets judged to be based on facts.

The internet blew up this model, for better and worse. For better, it has become more and more difficult for authoritarian leaders to control the information their societies receive and to disseminate lies unchallenged. The internet is too valuable a medium of commerce and interpersonal connection to ban, but the vast quantity of information flowing on it every moment of every day makes it difficult if not impossible to regulate.[17] For worse, people and groups seeking to influence people in ways that would promote their goals now have a ready way to mislead and inflame others by presenting them with false information, fake news that may seem genuine to a credulous mind.

Now comes AI, with a more persuasive way of creating fake news than has ever been possible before. We are vulnerable to fake news in part because we are a generally credulous species, prone to creating and accepting imaginary realities, as we have seen abundantly in previous chapters.[18] But AI-generated fake news is even more persuasive than other forms of imaginary reality, because we have an especially strong tendency to believe what we see, even more than we tend to believe what we hear or read. In psychological research this is called the "realism heuristic," and it is well-established in experimental psychological research.[19] Even when a deepfake is so far from a political figure's known statements that viewers are skeptical that it is real, the deepfake has the effect of undermining the political figure's legitimacy and negatively influencing people's opinions. So you may have suspected Zelenskyy's surrender statement was not believable because it was contrary to everything he had said before . . . and yet your trust in him may have been undermined anyway, whether or not you consciously realized it.

Now that it is not only possible but technologically simple for AI to show people doing and saying things they never did or said and to show events happening that never happened, the potential for political uses of inflammatory deception is enormous.[20] Political and religious tensions between nations and communities could be ignited by depicting outgroup members committing acts of destruction or desecration of the ingroup's cherished symbols or places. Elections could be swayed by circulating a last-minute deepfake of a false but deeply offensive video of one of the competitors being "exposed" doing or saying something outrageous or disgraceful. Financial markets could be disrupted by having a deepfake show a trusted figure issuing an imminent prediction of catastrophic events. Military conflicts could be generated by deepfakes showing that an attack by enemies has begun or is about to begin, thus triggering a sudden preemptive attack against a threat that never existed. All of these deepfakes could be distributed lightning-fast through social media networks that are next to impossible to shut down or control.

As people become more familiar with deepfakes, they will become more skeptical of what they see and hear on the internet, but this creates another kind of problem: deepfakes may undermine public trust in *everything* people see and hear from public figures.[21] Could be real; could be a deepfake. Since you never know what is real and what is fake, it may be best to assume that everything you see and hear from public figures may be false (Figure 7.3). This mistrust results in the Liar's Dividend, as the most unscrupulous liars exploit public skepticism to deny that they have done and said what they actually did and said. "Fake news!" the liar cries when caught red-handed committing well-documented offenses. Sound familiar?

Our propensity for embracing imaginary realities makes us seriously vulnerable to deepfakes. We are already not very adept at distinguishing what is happening around us from what we expect to happen and what we wish would happen and what we fear might happen. To put it another way, we are all too adept at reshaping and transforming everything we experience so that it fits comfortably with the imaginary reality we have constructed that allows us to believe we understand the world around us and know how to act within that world with confidence.

And yet, paradoxically, we simultaneously seek to discern *what is really happening* in the world and how we can use that knowledge to decide what to do next. So, for example, in our hunter-gatherer history, if an animal we had mainly relied on for food suddenly seemed scarce, we would have desperately sought an explanation, often guided by our imaginary reality. The gods were punishing us for our misbehavior or our failure to worship them adequately, so we must change our ways and offer more and better sacrifices. But at the same time we would explore places where our main prey source may have gone and seek out other possible sources of sustenance until the gods relented.

Figure 7.3 Kamala Harris never called herself "the ultimate diversity hire," but it is easy to find a deepfake video of her supposedly doing so.

Similarly, deepfakes exploit the fears and anxieties and hopes that shape our imaginary realities, precisely because they seem to be revealing *what is really happening* that has so far been concealed from us. They falsify at the same time as they persuade us that they are revealing what is true. Psychological research has long established that people generally have a "trust-default"; that is, they tend to believe what they see and hear and assume that others can be trusted in the information they provide.[22] Throughout human history, the trust-default has been perpetually exploited to deceive and mislead, but deepfakes represent a new and dangerously effective form of exploitation, because they seem so real. There it is, right before your own eyes and ears. How could it not be real, especially if it accords with something you already suspect or that you deeply want to believe?

So what can be done to thwart the mischief of deepfakes? Researchers and observers on this topic advocate education as the answer.[23] People can be educated about the novel deceptive techniques employed in deepfakes. They can be warned about the signs that something is a deepfake and encouraged to seek out other sources to confirm or disconfirm it. But this is a vain strategy, a pipe dream. Who will contradict the deepfake you have just watched when you are within your information silo with others who believe what you do and whose beliefs are also encouraged and reinforced by the deepfake? Sure, you could seek out contrary sources of information that would disconfirm the story told in the deepfake, but why should you, when the deepfake is so psychologically rewarding and fits so nicely within the imaginary reality you already have?

As bad as all this sounds, there is an aspect of AI that is even worse. There is a formidable, dangerous brew possible, even likely, that mixes our tendency for imaginary realities, the deepfakes that exploit this tendency, and our possession of weapons of mass destruction. Think of the world's most volatile potential conflicts: China and Taiwan, Israel and Iran, India and Pakistan, and innumerable other current conflicts within and between states all over the world. What will happen when AI deepfakes are used to depict the military leaders of one side in these conflicts being engaged in planning an imminent attack on their adversaries? How will we prevent a crisis of deception and misperception in these circumstances from leading to a catastrophic conflict? Keep in mind, too, that deepfakes were first invented only a few years ago and they have already become much more convincing than they were at first, much more difficult to distinguish from a real video. They are sure to get even better in the future.

Is there an effective way to address the incendiary threat that deepfakes could trigger massive conflict? We will have to rely on the institutional safeguards that have developed over the past century, specifically established media outlets and intergovernmental associations. The established media outlets, that is, the oft-derided "legacy media" that have existed for decades and have established at least a decent if not unblemished reputation for integrity, can refute the lies promoted in deepfakes. But will enough people believe them in an era when their credibility is constantly attacked and when increasing numbers of people ignore them and get their news from unvetted social media sources? And can't the judgments of the legacy media be deepfaked, too? As for the intergovernmental associations, such as the United Nations, they have helped mediate and defuse many potential conflicts over the decades they have existed. But will they have enough power to intervene in case of potential catastrophes, and will their authority and credibility be respected by all sides when a conflict is about to begin?

I wish I had answers to these questions, but the fact is that AI is a near-perfect technology for exploiting our collective weakness for the allure of imaginary realities. Stopping its influence would require either well-crafted worldwide regulations or universal education capable of enabling us to overcome our most fundamental psychology. I fear we may be in for some tough times in this domain. I hope I am wrong.

Defeating Death? Our Biomedical Future

It is not only AI that represents a new technology with exciting possibilities as well as unsettling threats. New breakthroughs in recent years in our understanding of genetics and the biological processes involved in aging hold an unprecedented promise for us to extend the human lifespan further than ever before—and not only the lifespan but the *health span*, the number of years that we remain lucid and vigorous.[24] Most notably, gene editing using CRISPR technology has raised formidable questions about how much we could change our genome—and whether we should. Research is just beginning in this area, but the possibilities are both thrilling and disturbing. The century ahead is certain to reveal many answers to questions about how to change and extend the course of individual development in profound ways, and each century beyond that will expand further our ability to alter it.

There is much more than CRISPR happening in research on ways to slow or stall or reverse the processes of aging. I don't want to go into the details here of the biomedical research on aging, because my focus is on the psychological consequences of extending the lifespan and health span, and in any case biomedical research is in constant motion and new findings come out daily. The important point here is that it is clear that the processes involved in aging are being identified and ways are being developed to slow down or reverse those processes.

How will new biomedical advances alter our psychological development? How will we adjust to radically different expectations for the human life course? It is difficult to predict just how long a healthy human will eventually be able to live, but a conservative estimate would be that by the end of the 21st century most people will stay healthy past age 100. Yet all of our traditional cultural and psychological expectations for the arc of the life course are based on a much different model, lasting a total of maybe 70 or 80 years: childhood and youth to about age 20, adult duties and responsibilities for 30 to 40 years, then a couple of decades of late adulthood characterized by physical and mental decline and withdrawal.[25] How will it change our perceptions and beliefs about human development and about ourselves once it is possible to remain not only alive but healthy as ever through a century of life or more?

There are many good reasons for optimism about our biomedical future, given how our unique abilities for accumulating scientific knowledge and developing technologies have already transformed our lives for the better in so many ways. Nevertheless, as the chapters in this book show, we also have a dangerous tendency to delude ourselves in ways that often harm others and ultimately ourselves. That tendency will not go away, no matter how long we live or how healthy we remain. Let us now discuss the possible psychological effects of our future biomedical advances, the threats as well as the benefits.

Forever Young? Be Careful What You Wish For

Among the Trobriand Islanders, the traditional cultural belief is that death is not the end of life but the entry to a pleasant and leisurely afterlife.[26] The people believe that after death the spirit (*baloma*) is transported to Tuma, the Island of the Dead, where life continues much as before, only with less work and more enjoyment. Although aging occurs on Tuma, when people become old baloma merely bathes in the sea, sloughs off the aged, wrinkled skin, and is rejuvenated as a fresh, virile youth. After a few cycles of this, baloma returns to the land of the living and is reincarnated in the family lineage, entering through the head of the mother.

Sounds pretty good, right? Who wouldn't want to be rejuvenated now and then as a fresh, virile youth every time aging begins to rear its ugly head and make us weaker, slower, wrinklier, and . . . less virile. If you were offered a pill right now that would return you to your physical state at age 25, and keep you there indefinitely, would you take it (Figure 7.4)?

I am not sure how I personally would answer that question. I loved being age 25; I remember it well. I felt physically invincible and cognitively on fire, and I am sure I was better looking then than I have been in any year since.

Still, I don't long to return to that psychological state—which is also a physical state, so it would inevitably go along with being returned physically to age 25. I felt invincible, all right—to a dangerous degree. I did a lot of stupid things that were motivated by that assumption of invincibility—and by a corresponding excess of testosterone, no doubt, which also peaks around age 25. I could have died or killed others with my carelessness, many times, so many I shudder to think about them. At age 68, as I write this, I may

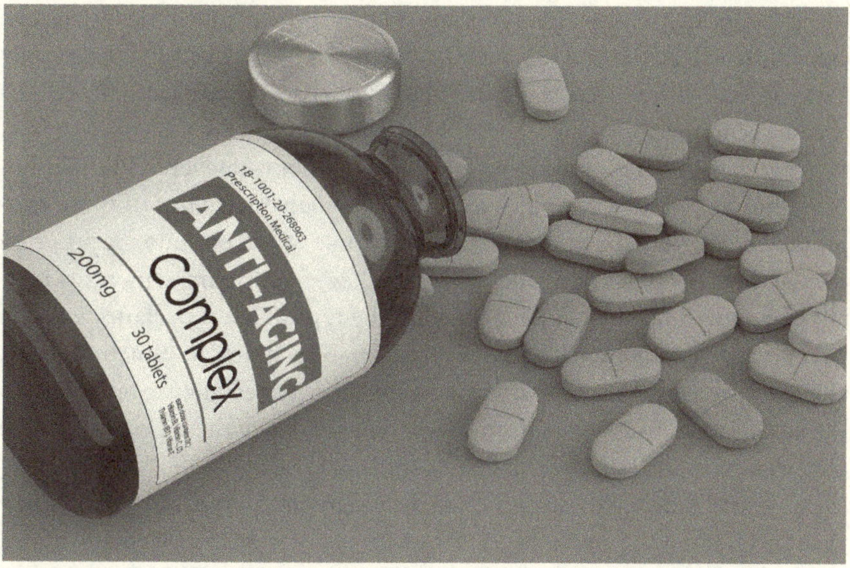

Figure 7.4 If there were a pill that would return you physically to age 25 indefinitely, would you take it?

not be a virile youth any more, but I am certainly wiser and more considerate of others.

So before you answer yes to this hypothetical offer of immortality, consider this. Assume that if you could take a pill that would return you physically to age 25, it would also return you psychologically to age 25, because the physical is the basis of the psychological. Would you want your 25-year-old personality again? That means you would be just as impulsive as you were at age 25, just as prone to anger, tears, and other emotional extremes as you were then, because all the hormones that drive those emotions would be at the age-25 level, not the cooler levels that they steadily descend through beyond age 25. Those hormones would also drive your judgment. Do you make better decisions now than you did at age 25? I ask this question all the time in the public lectures I give, so I know the answer is yes for the overwhelming majority of people who are over age 30. Would you give up better emotional control and better judgment in order to return yourself to the physical state of a virile youth?

Then consider the societal changes that would occur once living indefinitely is available to everyone. Of course, it won't be everyone at first. Like all new technological advances, it will be available first to the rich. So, all the arrogant rich billionaire SOBs you detest who are now in the public eye constantly will be the first to benefit. Swell. But it seems likely that eventually everyone will have access to the new pill, just as everyone eventually gained access to indoor plumbing, electric lighting, and automobiles.

What then? Better forget about Social Security or whatever public pension program you were planning to rely upon in your dotage. All of those programs were designed on the premise that people would pay into the program during their entire working life in order to have a few years of monthly benefit payments after they finally retired. If the typical life expectancy extends beyond age 100, there will be no way for those programs to remain solvent; already they are teetering under the strain of life expectancy extending into the 80s, more than 20 years beyond where it was when these programs were first created in the late 19th and early 20th centuries.

For years I taught a lifespan human development course, and when I came to the section on the end of life, I would ask my students, "How many of you would like to live to be 120?" Almost all hands went up. Then I would ask, "Okay, what if living to 120 meant that you had to work until you are 100, would you still want to live that long?" Almost all hands went down.

How about you?

There are certainly plenty of literary and historical warnings against the hubris of trying to achieve human immortality. Should we heed them? Over two millennia ago the Greeks told the instructive story of Sisyphus. You probably know that Sisyphus was condemned to roll a boulder up a hill, whereupon it would roll down again, and he would have to roll it up there again and again, forever. But the full story is much more compelling. Sisyphus's eternal labor was punishment for his attempt to achieve immortality. He tied up Thanatos, the god of death, and rendered him powerless. Hooray, right? Not exactly. Now NOTHING died. Animals could not be consumed for food. The old and sick could not put an end to their suffering. Plus, the other gods were deeply offended by Sisyphus's hubris. How dare he assume the power of the gods? So they released Thanatos, restoring the balance between death and life, and gave Sisyphus the punishment they believed he deserved.

Shortly after the myth of Sisyphus was created came the instructive historical tale of Qin Shi Huang, the first emperor of China, who ordered all the wisest scholars and magicians to devote themselves to inventing a potion that would keep him alive forever. When they presented him with the results of all their efforts, he promptly dropped dead—because the potion contained mercury, a marvelous substance but not one you should drink if you want to stay healthy, much less live forever.

Closer to our own time, in the early days of the Soviet Union a group calling themselves the God Builders (seriously) sought to find a way to reverse the aging process. They concluded that the answer would be to give aged people infusions of the blood of young people. One of their leaders, Alexander Bogdanov, made himself the subject of one of these early experiments, whereupon—this will not surprise you by now—he died from a botched blood transfusion.[27]

Well, maybe this is all a lot of fearmongering designed to provoke Anxiety-Prone Threat Detectors like us. Maybe all these attempts to prolong life will work out for the best. Maybe we will extend the lifespan as well as the health span indefinitely, making us all much happier than we are now, given that all of us have a fear of death. But if you have read this far in this book, you will not be surprised to learn that my conclusion is not quite so optimistic. On the contrary, because of the many ways we imagine and distort reality, any benefits that result from learning to delay or reverse aging processes are likely to be mixed in their effects, if not purely disastrous.

Conquering death is a long-standing human aspiration, probably as old as humanity. It is this wish that led us to create so many fabulous imaginary realities of a pleasurable afterlife lasting forever. So it is doubtful that we would be able to resist the temptation to prolong life indefinitely if we were able to achieve it. Not only that, but our moral egoism will surely be invoked to defend our *right* to live forever. God must *want* us to live forever, otherwise we would never have been allowed to develop the technologies that would enable us to do so. Or at least God must want *some* of us to live forever. Our group, obviously. Your group? Hmmmm, that doesn't seem like nearly so good an idea.

One Final Story

I have often drawn on stories and myths in this book, and I will end the book with the story of Pandora's Box as a cautionary tale. This is another story you have probably heard of but may not know in detail. In the Greek myth, Zeus gives Pandora a special box in order to punish humanity after Prometheus gave them the fire stolen from the gods. Pandora is told only that it contains wondrous gifts from the gods—and she is instructed not to open it, ever!

But she does, of course, and releases not gifts but curses: disease, death, and myriad other unnamed evils.

The message of Pandora's Box is that what seems like a great gift can sometimes turn out to be a curse—and that by the time we discover it is a curse, it may be too late. We may be living in a Pandora's Box era. Our spectacular achievements in niche construction, AI, and anti-aging research all seem like marvelous gifts—but may eventually morph into curses that bring us down. The powers we have developed are dangerous in a species so prone to imaginary realities. My hope is that this book, especially this chapter, will help alert us to the perils planted deep in the psychology of human nature, and the necessity of recognizing them to prevent irreparable damage to the future of our unique species and all the species that are threatened by us. Our imaginary realities represent our amazing psychological ability to transform suffering and perplexity into comfort and even bliss. The challenge before us, now and forever more, is to use that ability in ways that avoid its potentials for generating conflict, cruelty, and destruction, and instead master it in ways that generate creativity and compassion.

Notes

Preface

1. Fromm (1973).
2. Freud (1917/1966).
3. Nietzsche (1884/1966).
4. Harari (2015).
5. Vyse (2022).
6. Gottschall (2021).
7. *The Key to All Mythologies* is the life's work of Edward Casaubon in George Eliot's *Middlemarch.* Throughout Eliot's novel, Casaubon talks about this book and his devotion to it and all the work he is supposedly doing on it, but after he marries Dorothea, she discovers he has never written a thing, only taken notes on others' works, for decades. He drops dead before finishing it—before even starting it, really. Ever since, *The Key to All Mythologies* has been a kind of shorthand, both tragic and ridiculous, to symbolize the vanity of academics.

Chapter 1

1. This is the title of Roy Baumeister's (2005) excellent book, so I am happy to give him credit for coining the term. Also see Henrich (2015).
2. For example, Buss (2019); Tooby (2020). There is a lot to be learned from evolutionary psychology, but we certainly differ on what classifies as "culture."
3. Kitayama and Salvador (2024); Shweder (1991).
4. Laland et al. (2016).
5. Wrangham (2009). This fascinating book focuses on how the control of fire shaped human brain development.
6. Gazzaniga (2012).
7. Berger (2012).
8. Vyse (2022).
9. Gottschall (2021). Gottschall does a terrific job of detailing the delusional potential of our story-making abilities.
10. Brown (2004).
11. Cooper (2019); Festinger (1959).
12. Baumeister (2005).
13. C. Smith (2018).
14. McLean and Syed (2016). Also see Schiff (2017). Hammack (2008) is another eloquent theorist on master and personal narratives. See Freeman (2003) for a thoughtful essay on the relations between narratives and truth.
15. For example, McAdams (2013); Perlin and Fivush (2021).

Chapter 2

1. Vyse (2013).
2. Subbotsky (2010).
3. Brashier and Multhaup (2017).
4. Woolley et al. (2011).
5. Nemeroff and Rozin (1989).
6. Gecewicz (2018).
7. Hays (2014).
8. T. Smith (1996).
9. Hutson (2010).
10. Volz and Gazzaniga (2017).

11. Meissner et al. (2011).
12. Moore and Fresco (2012).
13. Turnbull (2015).
14. Durkheim (2016).
15. Rossano (2010); Van Bavel and Packer (2021).
16. Tomasello (2019).
17. Tomasello (2019).
18. Hellmer et al. (2021).
19. Tomasello (2019).
20. Arnett (1998).
21. Dubourg and Baumard (2022). They use the term "imaginary worlds," but I think "fictional worlds" fits better what they describe.
22. Jensen (1998).
23. Von Hippel & Trivers (2011); Vyse (2022).
24. Gottschall (2021). His book is an excellent analysis of both the constructive and destructive forms of our tendency for constructing imaginary realities.
25. Arnett and Jensen (2015).

Chapter 3

1. Wallace (2018).
2. Ridley (2010); Tierney and Baumeister (2019).
3. Rozin and Royzman (2001).
4. Bowlby and Solomon (1989).
5. LoBue et al. (2019).
6. Ballard (2019); Suter (2024). In the survey reported by Ballard, 45% of Americans believed in ghosts; in the survey reported by Suter, it was 61%.
7. Suter (2024).
8. Chapman University (2023).
9. Bricker (2019).
10. Vyse (2013).
11. Bates and Turner (2003).
12. Vyse (2013).
13. Berger (2012).
14. Radcliffe-Brown (2014).
15. Van der Meer et al. (2020). This paper provides a good review of research on how media content stokes anxieties.
16. Stubbersfield et al. (2015).
17. Gerbner et al. (1986).
18. Tierney and Baumeister (2019).
19. Grignolio (2018).
20. Orth (2023); Uscinski and Parent (2014).
21. Douglas et al. (2019); Ma-Kellams (2015).
22. Douglas et al. (2019).
23. Douglas et al. (2019).
24. Dubourg and Baumard (2022).
25. Arnett (1994a); Zuckerman (2007).

Chapter 4

1. Fishman (2010).
2. Frost (1977).
3. Marcos (1998).
4. Cooper (2019); Festinger (1959).
5. Aronson (1997); Tavris and Aronson (2015).
6. Tavris and Aronson (2015).
7. Gray and Silver (1990).
8. Tavris and Aronson (2015).
9. Suls et al. (2019); Zell et al. (2020).
10. Klein and Epley (2016).

11. Baumeister et al. (1990).
12. Preuss and Alicke (2017).
13. De Freitas et al. (2017); Strohminger et al. (2017).
14. Sedikides et al. (2014).
15. Benson et al. (2017).
16. Stadler and Benson (2012); Sykes and Matza (1957). Recently an alternative term, "moral disengagement," has been proposed (Bandura, 2016; Bussey, 2020), but it has the same limitations as "neutralization."
17. Bandura (2016); Bilali and Vollhardt (2019); Bussey (2020); Sykes and Matza (1957); Stadler and Benson (2012).
18. Sedikides et al. (2014).
19. Malti et al. (2020).
20. Gutzwiller-Helfinger et al. (2010).
21. Arnett (2008); Thalmayer et al. (2021).
22. Bellah et al. (1985); Putnam (2000). Some have made the case that individualism really begins with the Protestant Reformation in the early 16th century, well before the Enlightenment, but I think the Enlightenment is a more definite beginning.
23. Heywood (2017); Stearns (2005).
24. Caplow (1982).
25. Whiting et al. (1988).
26. Luther (2018).
27. Luther (2018).
28. Tajfel (1978, 2010).
29. Bilali and Vollhardt (2019); Slovic et al. (2020).
30. Parker and Janoff-Bulman (2013).
31. Gur (2025).
32. Jefferson (1807).
33. Jackson (1833).
34. Arnett (1995); Markus and Kitayama (2010).
35. Anderson (2017).
36. Pinker (2011).
37. Arnett (2002).
38. Santos et al. (2017).

Chapter 5

1. Bowlby (2012).
2. Pickering (1984).
3. Panksepp (2005) is a good representative of this view.
4. Panksepp (2005). It is not clear to me how anyone could tell that a rat chirp reflects positive emotional feelings.
5. Henrich (2015).
6. Rogoff (2003).
7. Lifton (2019).
8. Fitch (2017).
9. Brown (2004).
10. Costa et al. (2022).
11. Campbell (2010).
12. Arnett (1994b).
13. Arnett (2017).
14. Duffy and Mair (2017); Ehrenreich (2006).
15. Arnett (2017).
16. R. Smith (2013).
17. Brambilla and Riva (2017).
18. Ouwerkerk et al. (2018).
19. Singh (2018).
20. Singh (2018).
21. Vandereycken and Deth (1994).
22. Merback (2007).

23. R. Smith and van Dijk (2018).
24. Ehrenreich (2006).
25. Williams (1865).
26. Darwin (2001).
27. Masten (2015).
28. McAdams et al. (2001).

Chapter 6

1. Miczo (2022).
2. Kramer (2015).
3. Ford (2015).
4. Hodson and MacInnis (2016).
5. Martin and Ford (2018); Miczo (2022).
6. Martin and Ford (2018).
7. Martin and Ford (2018). Humor researchers call this a "humor mindset," but I like "humor readiness" better, because it is more than a cognitive disposition; it is also social and emotional.
8. Hodson and MacInnis (2016).
9. Martin and Ford (2018).
10. Lawless et al. (2020).
11. Miczo (2022).
12. Ford et al. (2008).
13. Pérez (2016).
14. Kramer (2015).
15. Martin and Ford (2018).
16. Kramer (2015).
17. Corbeill (2015).
18. Hopper (2016).
19. Hopper (2016).
20. Smirnova (2014).
21. Yegerov (2019).
22. Yegerov (2019).
23. Stent (2024).
24. Ford and Olah, 2021; Pérez (2016).
25. Frierson (2020).
26. Navasky (2013).
27. Friedman and Friedman (2024).

Chapter 7

1. United Nations Development Programme (2023).
2. *Investor's Business Daily* (2017).
3. Thomas (1983).
4. Harvard Business School (2024).
5. United Nations (2024).
6. Crutzen and Schwägerl (2021).
7. Amnesty International (2019).
8. Organisation for Economic Co-operation and Development (2024). Go to this link to find the percentage of women and men with tertiary educational attainment; in most countries, women have the advantage, especially in developed countries: https://www.compareyourcountry.org/education-at-a-glance-2021/en/1/3012+3013+3014+3021+3023/default.
9. Singer (2011).
10. Harari (2024b).
11. Hancock and Bailenson (2021).
12. Tiku (2024).
13. Harari (2024a). Harari may be over the top in his warnings about the supposed dangers of AI, but he has a lot of thoughtful observations to share on the new technology in this book.
14. Bellware (2024).
15. Karasavva and Noorbhai (2021); Nelson (2024).
16. Hiebert (2022).

17. North Korea may be the only country to have successfully banned the internet, but at the cost of deep economic misery. China bans Google but has its own, state-controlled browser.
18. Hameleers et al. (2024).
19. Hameleers et al. (2024).
20. Busch and Ware (2023); Gambín et al. (2024).
21. Hancock and Bailenson (2021).
22. Hameleers et al. (2024).
23. Busch and Ware (2023).
24. Pan (2024).
25. Arnett (2017).
26. Arnett (2017).
27. Nikiforuk (2024).

References

Amnesty International. (2019). *Generation Z ranks climate change highest as vital issue of our time.* https://www.amnestyusa.org/press-releases/generation-z-ranks-climate-change-highest-as-vital-issue-of-our-time-in-amnesty-international-survey/#:~:text=Across%20the%2022%20countries%20at,violence%20against%20women%20(21%25)

Anderson, K. (2017). "Who was I to stop the killing?" Moral neutralization among Rwandan genocide perpetrators. *Journal of Perpetrator Research, 1*, 39–63.

Arnett, J. (1994a). Sensation seeking: A new conceptualization and a new scale. *Personality and Individual Differences, 16*(2), 289–296.

Arnett, J. (1994b). *Metalheads: Heavy metal music and adolescent alienation.* Routledge.

Arnett, J. J. (1995). Broad and narrow socialization: The family in the context of a cultural theory. *Journal of Marriage and the Family, 57*, 617–628.

Arnett, J. J. (1998). Learning to stand alone: The contemporary American transition to adulthood in cultural and historical context. *Human Development, 41*(5–6), 295–315.

Arnett, J. J. (2002). The psychology of globalization. *American Psychologist, 57*, 774–783.

Arnett, J. J. (2008). The neglected 95%: Why American psychology needs to become less American. *American Psychologist, 63*(7), 602–614.

Arnett, J. J. (2017). Life stage concepts across history and cultures: Proposal for a new field on Indigenous life stages. *Human Development, 59*(5), 290–316.

Arnett, J. J., & Jensen, L. A. (2015). "There's more between heaven and earth." Danish emerging adults' religious beliefs and values. *Journal of Adolescent Research, 30*(6), 661–682.

Aronson, E. (1997). Back to the future: Retrospective review of Leon Festinger's—A theory of cognitive dissonance. *American Journal of Psychology, 110*(1), 127.

Ballard, J. (2019). *Many Americans believe ghosts and demons exist.* YouGov. https://today.yougov.com/society/articles/25908-paranormal-beliefs-ghosts-demons-poll?redirect_from=%2Ftopics%2Flifestyle%2Farticles-reports%2F2019%2F10%2F21%2Fparanormal-beliefs-ghosts-demons-poll

Bandura, A. (2016). *Moral disengagement: How people do harm and live with themselves.* Worth.

Bates, B., & Turner, A. N. (2003). Imagery and symbolism in the birth practices of traditional cultures. In L. Dundes (Ed.), *The manner born: Birth rites in cross-cultural perspective* (pp. 85–97). AltaMira Press.

Baumeister, R. F. (2005). *The cultural animal: Human nature, meaning, and social life.* Oxford.

Baumeister, R. F., Stillwell, A., & Wotman, S. R. (1990). Victim and perpetrator accounts of interpersonal conflict: Autobiographical narratives about anger. *Journal of Personality and Social Psychology, 59*, 994–1005.

Bégouën, H., & Breuil, H. (1920). Un dessin relevé dans la grotte des Trois Frères à Montesquieu-Avantès (Ariège). Comptes rendus des séances de l'Académie des Inscriptions et Belles-Lettres, *303*, 45.

Bellah, R. N., Madsen, R., Sullivan, W. M., Swidler, A., & Tipton, S. M. (1985). *Habits of the heart: Individualism and commitment in American life.* University of California Press.

Bellware, K. (2024, October 24). Her teenage son killed himself after talking to a chatbot. *Washington Post.* https://www.washingtonpost.com/nation/2024/10/24/character-ai-lawsuit-suicide/

Benson, M. L., & Cullen, F. T. (2017). Subterranean values, self-deception, and white-collar crime. In T. G. Blomberg, F. T. Cullen, C. Carlsson, & C. L. Jonson (Eds.), *Delinquency and drift revisited* (vol. 21, pp. 99–124). Routledge.

Berger, A. S. (2012). The evil eye: An ancient superstition. *Journal of Religion and Health, 51*, 1098–1103.

Bilali, R., & Vollhardt, J. R. (2019). Victim and perpetrator groups' divergent perspectives on collective violence: Implications for intergroup relations. *Political Psychology, 40*, 75–108.

Bowlby, J. (2012). *The making and breaking of affectional bonds.* Routledge.

Bowlby, J., & Solomon, M. (1989). *Attachment theory.* Lifespan Learning Institute.

Brambilla, M., & Riva, P. (2017). Predicting pleasure at others' misfortune: Morality trumps sociability and competence in driving deservingness and schadenfreude. *Motivation and Emotion, 41*(2), 243–253.

Brashier, N. M., & Multhaup, K. S. (2017). Magical thinking decreases across adulthood. *Psychology and Aging, 32*(8), 681.

Bricker, D. (2019). *World affairs: Citizens in 28 countries assess engagement in international affairs for a global perspective.* International Security Forum.

Brown, D. E. (2004). Human universals, human nature and human culture. *Daedalus, 133*(4), 47–54.

Busch, E., & Ware, J. (2023). *The weaponization of deepfakes: Digital deception by the far right.* International Centre for Counter-Terrorism. chrome-extension://efaidnbmnnnibpcajpcglclefindmkaj/https://icct.nl/sites/default/files/2023-12/The%20Weaponisation%20of%20Deepfakes.pdf

Buss, D. (2019). *Evolutionary psychology: The new science of the mind.* Routledge.

Bussey, K. (2020). Development of moral disengagement. In L. A. Jensen (Ed.), *The Oxford handbook of moral development: An interdisciplinary perspective* (pp. 306–333). Oxford University Press.

Campbell, P. S. (2010). *Songs in their heads: Music and its meaning in children's lives.* Oxford University Press.

Caplow, T. (1982). *Middletown families: Fifty years of change and continuity.* University of Minnesota Press.

Chapman University. (2023). *Chapman University survey of American fears.* https://blogs.chapman.edu/wilkinson/2023/10/20/the-top-10-fears-in-american-2023/

Cooper, J. (2019). Cognitive dissonance: Where we've been and where we're going. *International Review of Social Psychology, 32*, 1–11. https://doi.org/10.5334/irsp.277

Corbeill, A. (2015). *Controlling laughter: Political humor in the late Roman Republic.* Princeton University Press.

Costa, V. S., Bündchen, D. C., Sousa, H., Pires, L. B., & Felipetti, F. A. (2022). Clinical benefits of music-based interventions on preterm infants' health: A systematic review of randomised trials. *Acta Paediatrica, 111*(3), 478–489.

Crutzen, P. J., & Schwägerl, C. (2021). Living in the Anthropocene: Toward a new global ethos. In S. Benner, G. Lax, P. J. Crutzen, U. Pöschl, J. Lelieveld, & H. G. Brauch (Eds.), *Paul J. Crutzen and the Anthropocene: A new epoch in earth's history* (pp. 141–144). Springer. (Original work published 2011).

Darwin, C. (2001). *The voyage of the Beagle: Journal of researches into the natural history and geology of the countries visited during the voyage of HMS Beagle round the world.* Modern Library.

De Freitas, J., Cikara, M., Grossmann, I., & Schlegel, R. (2017). Origins of the belief in good true selves. *Trends in Cognitive Sciences, 21*(9), 634–636.

Douglas, K. M., Uscinski, J. E., Sutton, R. M., Cichocka, A., Nefes, T., Ang, C. S., & Deravi, F. (2019). Understanding conspiracy theories. *Advances in Political Psychology, 40*, 3–35.

Dubourg, E., & Baumard, N. (2022). Why imaginary worlds? The psychological foundations and cultural evolution of fictions with imaginary worlds. *Behavioral and Brain Sciences, 45*, e276.

Duffy, M., & Mair, J. (2017). *Festival encounters: Theoretical perspectives on festival events.* Routledge.

Durkheim, É. (2016). The elementary forms of religious life. In *Social theory re-wired* (pp. 52–67). Routledge.

Ehrenreich, B. (2006). *Dancing in the streets: A history of collective joy.* Metropolitan.

Festinger, L. (1959). *A theory of cognitive dissonance.* Stanford University Press.

Fishman, S. (2010, June 4). Bernie Madoff, Free at Last. *New York Magazine.* https://nymag.com/news/crimelaw/66468/#:~ text=But%20that%20evening%20an%20inmate,'m%20doing%20150%20yeavrs.%E2%80%9D

Fitch, W. T. (2017). Empirical approaches to the study of language evolution. *Psychonomic Bulletin & Review, 24*(1), 3–33.

Ford, T. E. (2015). The social consequences of disparagement humor: Introduction and overview. *Humor, 28*(2), 163–169.

Ford, T. E., Boxer, C. F., Armstrong, J., & Edel, J. R. (2008). More than "just a joke": The prejudice-releasing function of sexist humor. *Personality and Social Psychology Bulletin, 34*(2), 159–170.

Ford, T. E., & Olah, A. R. (2021). Disparagement humor and prejudice. In M. Strick & T. E. Ford (Eds.), *The social psychology of humor* (pp 171–186). Routledge.

Freeman, M. (2003). Rethinking the fictive, reclaiming the real: Autobiography, narrative time, and the burden of truth. In G. D. Fireman, T. E. McVay, & O. J. Flanagan (Eds.), *Narrative and consciousness: Literature, psychology, and the brain* (pp. 115–128). Oxford University Press.

Freud, S. (1917/1966). *Introductory lectures on psychoanalysis.* Norton.

Friedman, L. W., & Friedman, H. H. (2024). Jewish humor as a survival tool and a bridge to social justice. In O. Feldman (Ed.), *Political humor worldwide: The cultural context of political comedy, satire, and parody* (pp. 139–157). Springer Nature Singapore.

Frierson, M. (2020). *Freedom in laughter: Dick Gregory, Bill Cosby, and the civil rights movement.* SUNY Press.

Fromm, E. (1973). *The anatomy of human destructiveness.* Macmillan.

Frost, D. (1977). Interview with Richard Nixon. *The Guardian.* https://www.theguardian.com/theguardian/2007/sep/07/greatinterviews1#:~:text=Now%2C%20I%20can%20be%20faulted,them%20off%20in%20that%20way.

Gambín, Á. F., Yazidi, A., Vasilakos, A., Haugerud, H., & Djenouri, Y. (2024). Deepfakes: Current and future trends. *Artificial Intelligence Review, 57*(3), 64.

Gazzaniga, M. S. (Ed.). (2012). *Neuropsychology.* Springer Science & Business Media.

Gecewicz, C. (2018, October 1). *"New Age" beliefs common among both religious and non-religious Americans.* Pew Research Center. https://www.pewresearch.org/short-reads/2018/10/01/new-age-beliefs-common-among-both-religious-and-nonreligious-americans/

Gerbner, G., Gross, L., Morgan, M., & Signorielli, N. (1986). Living with television: The dynamics of the cultivation process. In J. Bryant & D. Zillman (Eds.), *Perspectives on Media Effects* (pp. 17–40). Lawrence Erlbaum Associates.

Gottschall, J. (2021). *The story paradox: How our love of storytelling builds societies and tears them down.* Basic Books.

Gray, J. D., & Silver, R. C. (1990). Opposite sides of the same coin: Former spouses' divergent perspectives in coping with their divorce. *Journal of personality and Social Psychology, 59*(6), 1180.

Grignolio, A. (2018). *Vaccines: Are they worth a shot?* Springer.

Gur, T. E. (2025). 100 quotes by George Washington. Available: https://elevatesociety.com/quotes-by-george-washington/

Gutzwiller-Helfenfinger, E., Gasser, L., & Malti, T. (2010). Moral emotions and moral judgments in children's narratives: Comparing real-life and hypothetical transgressions. *New Directions for Child and Adolescent Development, 129*, 11–31.

Hameleers, M., van der Meer, T. G., & Dobber, T. (2024). Distorting the truth versus blatant lies: The effects of different degrees of deception in domestic and foreign political deepfakes. *Computers in Human Behavior, 152*, 108096.

Hammack, P. L. (2008). Narrative and the cultural psychology of identity. *Personality and Social Psychology Review, 12*(3), 222–247.

Hancock, J. T., & Bailenson, J. N. (2021). The social impact of deepfakes. *Cyberpsychology, Behavior, and Social Networking, 24*(3), 149–152.

Harari, Y. N. (2015). *Sapiens: A brief history of humankind.* Random House.

Harari, Y. N. (2024a). *Nexus: A brief history of information networks from the Stone Age to AI.* Random House.

Harari, Y. N. (2024b, September 4). What happens when the bots compete for your love? *Washington Post.* https://www.nytimes.com/2024/09/04/opinion/yuval-harari-ai-democracy.html

Harvard Business School. (2024). *What is the tragedy of the commons and 5 examples.* https://online.hbs.edu/blog/post/tragedy-of-the-commons-impact-on-sustainability-issues#:~:text=The%20tragedy%20of%20the%20commons%20refers%20to%20a%20situation%20in,British%20writer%20William%20Forster%20Lloyd

Hays, B. (2014, February 11). Majority of young adults think astrology is a science. UPI. https://www.upi.com/Science_News/2014/02/11/Majority-of-young-adults-think-astrology-is-a-science/5201392135954/

Hellmer, K., Stenberg, G., & Fawcett, C. (2021). How does preschoolers' conformity relate to parental style, anonymous sharing, and obedience? *International Journal of Developmental Science, 15*(3–4), 49–59.

Henrich, J. (2015). *The secret of our success: How culture is driving human evolution, domesticating our species, and making us smarter*. Princeton University Press.

Heywood, C. (2017). *A history of childhood*. John Wiley & Sons.

Hiebert, K. (2022, April 27). *Democracies are dangerously unprepared for deepfakes*. Centre for International Governance Innovation. https://www.cigionline.org/articles/democracies-are-dangerously-unprepared-for-deepfakes/

Hodson, G., & MacInnis, C. C. (2016). Derogating humor as a delegitimization strategy in intergroup contexts. *Translational Issues in Psychological Science, 2*(1), 63.

Hopper, E. (2016). Greatest cartooning coup of all time: The British cartoonist who persuaded everyone that Napoleon was short. *National Post*. https://nationalpost.com/news/world/greatest-cartooning-coup-of-all-time-the-brit-who-convinced-everyone-napoleon-was-short

Hutson, M. (2010). *The 7 laws of magical thinking: How irrational beliefs keep us happy, healthy, and sane*. Plume.

Investor's Business Daily. (2017, November 15). Al Gore's climate change hypocrisy is as big as his energy-sucking mansion. https://www.investors.com/politics/editorials/al-gores-climate-change-hypocrisy-is-as-big-as-his-energy-sucking-mansion/

Jackson, A. (1833, December 3). *Fifth Annual Message to Congress*. The American Presidency Project.

Jefferson, T. (1807, August 8). Letter from Thomas Jefferson to Henry Dearborn.

Jensen, L. A. (1998). Moral divisions within countries between orthodoxy and progressivism: India and the United States. *Journal for the Scientific Study of Religion, 37*, 90–107.

Karasavva, V., & Noorbhai, A. (2021). The real threat of deepfake pornography: A review of Canadian policy. *Cyberpsychology, Behavior, and Social Networking, 24*(3), 203–209.

Klein, N., & Epley, N. (2016). Maybe holier, but definitely less evil, than you: Bounded self-righteousness in social judgment. *Journal of Personality and Social Psychology, 110*(5), 660.

Kitayama, S., & Salvador, C. E. (2024). Cultural psychology: Beyond east and west. *Annual Review of Psychology, 75*(5:1–5), 32.

Kramer, C. A. (2015). *Subversive humor* [Unpublished doctoral dissertation]. Marquette University.

Laland, K., Matthews, B., & Feldman, M. W. (2016). An introduction to niche construction theory. *Evolutionary Ecology, 30*, 192–202.

Lawless, T. J., O'Dea, C. J., Miller, S. S., & Saucier, D. A. (2020). Is it really just a joke? Gender differences in perceptions of sexist humor. *Humor, 33*(2), 291–315.

Lifton, R. J. (2019). *Losing reality: On cults, cultism, and the mindset of political and religious zealotry*. New Press.

LoBue, V., Kim, E., & Delgado, M. (2019). Fear in development. In V. LoBue, K. Pérez-Edgar, & K. A. Buss (Eds.), *Handbook of emotional development* (pp. 257–282). Springer. https://doi.org/10.1007/978-3-030-17332-6_11

Luther, M. (2018). *The essential Luther*. Hackett Publishing.

Ma-Kellams, C. (2015). When perceiving the supernatural changes the natural: Religion and agency detection. *Journal of Cognition and Culture, 15*(3–4), 337–343.

Malti, T., Peplak, J., & Acland, E. (2020). Emotional experiences in moral contexts: Developmental perspectives. In L. A. Jensen (Ed.), *The Oxford handbook of moral development* (pp. 240–263). Oxford University Press.

Marcos, I. (1998). Wikiquote. https://en.wikiquote.org/wiki/Imelda_Marcos#:~:text=Times%20(1980).-,I%20was%20born%20ostentatious.,in%20%22Imelda%20(2003).

Markus, H. R., & Kitayama, S. (2010). Cultures and selves: A cycle of mutual constitution. *Perspectives on Psychological Science, 5*(4), 420–430.

Martin, R. A., & Ford, T. E. (2018). *The psychology of humor: An integrative approach* (2nd ed.). Academic Press.

Masten, A. S. (2015). *Ordinary magic: Resilience in development.* Guilford.

McAdams, D. P. (1993). *The stories we live by: Personal myths and the making of the self.* Guilford Press.

McAdams, D. P. (2013). *The redemptive self: Stories Americans live by* (Rev. ed.). Oxford University Press.

McAdams, D. P., Josselson, R. E., & Lieblich, A. E. (2001). *Turns in the road: Narrative studies of lives in transition.* American Psychological Association.

McLean, K. C., & Syed, M. (2016). Personal, master, and alternative narratives: An integrative framework for understanding identity development in context. *Human Development, 58*(6), 318–349.

Meissner, K., Bingel, U., Colloca, L., Wager, T. D., Watson, A., & Flaten, M. A. (2011). The placebo effect: Advances from different methodological approaches. *Journal of Neuroscience, 31*(45), 16117–16124.

Merback, M. B. (2007). Living image of pity: Mimetic violence, peace-making and salvific spectacle in the flagellant processions of the later Middle Ages. In D. H. Strickland (Ed.), *Images of medieval sanctity* (pp. 135–180). Brill.

Miczo, N. (2022). *Disparagement humor in social life: Competition vs. subjugation.* Rowman & Littlefield.

Moore, M. T., & Fresco, D. M. (2012). Depressive realism: A meta-analytic review. *Clinical Psychology Review, 32*(6), 496–509.

Navasky, V. S. (2013). *The art of controversy: Political cartoons and their enduring power.* Knopf.

Nelson, H. (2024, February 7). *Taylor Swift and the dangers of deepfake pornography.* National Sexual Violence Resource Center. https://www.nsvrc.org/blogs/feminism/taylor-swift-and-dangers-deepfake-pornography

Nemeroff, C., & Rozin, P. (1989). "You are what you eat": Applying the demand-free impressions technique to an unacknowledged belief. *Ethos, 17*(1), 50–69.

Nietzsche, F. W. (1966). *Thus spoke Zarathustra: A book for all and none* (W. Kaufmann, Trans.). Viking. (Original work published 1884)

Nietzsche, F. (2011). *The will to power.* Vintage.

Nikiforuk, A. (2024, December 10). *Ray Kurzweil, evangelist of techno-immortality.* Resilience. https://www.resilience.org/stories/2024-12-10/ray-kurzweil-evangelist-of-techno-immortality/

Organisation for Economic Co-operation and Development. (2024). *Compare your country.* https://www.compareyourcountry.org/education-at-a-glance-2021/en/1/3012+3013+3014+3021+3023/default

Orth, T. (2023). *Which conspiracy theories do Americans believe?* YouGov. https://today.yougov.com/politics/articles/48113-which-conspiracy-theories-do-americans-believe

Ouwerkerk, J. W., Van Dijk, W. W., Vonkeman, C. C., & Spears, R. (2018). When we enjoy bad news about other groups: A social identity approach to out-group schadenfreude. *Group Processes & Intergroup Relations, 21*(1), 214–232.

Pan, Y. (2024). New technologies and aging. *International Journal of Gerontology and Geriatric Medicine*, *1*(1), 31–30.

Panksepp, J. (2005). Beyond a joke: From animal laughter to human joy? *Science*, *308*(5718), 62–63.

Parker, M. T., & Janoff-Bulman, R. (2013). Lessons from morality-based social identity: The power of outgroup "hate," not just ingroup "love." *Social Justice Research*, *26*(1), 81–96.

Pérez, R. (2016). Racist humor: Then and now. *Sociology Compass*, *10*(10), 928–938.

Perlin, J. D., & Fivush, R. (2021). Revisiting redemption: A life span developmental account of the functions of narrative redemption. *Human Development*, *65*, 23–42.

Pickering, W. S. F. (1984). *Durkheim's sociology of religion*. Routledge and Kegan Paul.

Pinker, S. (2011). *The better angels of our nature: Why violence has declined*. Viking.

Preuss, G. S., & Alicke, M. D. (2017). My worst faults and misdeeds: Self-criticism and self-enhancement can co-exist. *Self and Identity*, *16*, 645–663.

Putnam, R. D. (2000). *Bowling alone: The collapse and revival of American community*. Simon and Schuster.

Radcliffe-Brown, A. R. (2014). *Taboo*. Cambridge University Press.

Ridley, M. (2010). *The rational optimist: How prosperity evolves*. Harper Perennial.

Rogoff, B. (2003). *The cultural nature of human development*. Oxford University Press.

Rossano, M. (2010). *Supernatural selection: How religion evolved*. Oxford University Press.

Rozin, P., & Royzman, E. B. (2001). Negativity bias, negativity dominance, and contagion. *Personality and Social Psychology Review*, *5*(4), 296–320.

Santos, H. C., Varnum, M. E., & Grossmann, I. (2017). Global increases in individualism. *Psychological Science*, *28*(9), 1228–1239.

Schiff, B. (2017). *A new narrative for psychology*. Oxford University Press.

Schopenhauer, A. (1970). *Essays and aphorisms*. Penguin UK.

Sedikides, C., Meek, R., Alicke, M. D., & Taylor, S. (2014). Behind bars but above the bar: Prisoners consider themselves more prosocial than non-prisoners. *British Journal of Social Psychology*, *53*(2), 396–403.

Shweder, R. A. (1991). *Thinking through cultures: Expeditions in cultural psychology*. Harvard University Press.

Singer, P. (2011). *The expanding circle: Ethics, evolution, and moral progress*. Princeton University Press.

Singh, M. (2018). The cultural evolution of shamanism. *Behavioral and Brain Sciences*, *41*, 1–16.

Slovic, P., Mertz, C. K., Markowitz, D. M., Quist, A., & Västfjäll, D. (2020). Virtuous violence from the war room to death row. *Proceedings of the National Academy of Sciences*, *117*(34), 20474–20482.

Smirnova, M. (2014). What is the shortest Russian joke? Communism. Russian cultural consciousness expressed through Soviet humor. *Qualitative Sociology*, *37*, 323–343.

Smith, C. (2018). *Atheist overreach: What atheism can't deliver*. Oxford University Press.

Smith, R. H. (2013). *The joy of pain: Schadenfreude and the dark side of human nature*. Oxford University Press.

Smith, R. H., & van Dijk, W. W. (2018). Schadenfreude and gluckschmerz. *Emotion Review*, *10*(4), 293–304.

Smith, T. W. (1996). *Environmental and scientific knowledge around the world*. National Opinion Research Center.

Stadler, W. A., & Benson, M. L. (2012). Revisiting the guilty mind: The neutralization of white-collar crime. *Criminal Justice Review, 37*(4), 494–511.

Stearns, P. N. (2005). *Growing up: The history of childhood in a global context* (vol. 28). Baylor University Press.

Steiner, G. (1984). *George Steiner: A reader*. Oxford University Press.

Stent, A. (2024, February 16). *The death of Alexei Navalny: Russia just lost its courageous opposition figure*. Brookings Institution. https://www.brookings.edu/articles/the-death-of-alexei-navalny/

Strohminger, N., Knobe, J., & Newman, G. (2017). The true self: A psychological concept distinct from the self. *Perspectives on Psychological Science, 12*(4), 551–560.

Stubbersfield, J. M., Tehrani, J. J., & Flynn, E. G. (2015). Serial killers, spiders and cybersex: Social and survival information bias in the transmission of urban legends. *British Journal of Psychology, 106*(2), 288–307.

Subbotsky, E. (2010). *Magic and the mind: Mechanisms, functions, and development of magical thinking and behavior*. Oxford University Press.

Suls, J., Collins, R. L., & Wheeler, L. (Eds.). (2019). *Social comparison, judgment, and behavior*. Oxford University Press.

Suter, T. (2024, January 10). Majorities of Americans believe in ghosts, aliens, the devil. *The Hill*. https://thehill.com/blogs/blog-briefing-room/4400922-americans-ghosts-aliens-devil-survey/#:~:text=Among%20those%20surveyed%2C%2056.9%20percent,say%20they%20believe%20in%20God

Sykes, G. M., & Matza, D. (1957). Techniques of neutralization: A theory of delinquency. *American Sociological Review, 22*, 664–670.

Tajfel, H. (Ed.) (1978). *Differentiation between social groups: Studies in the social psychology of intergroup relations*. Academic Press.

Tajfel, H. (Ed.). (2010). *Social identity and intergroup relations*. Cambridge University Press.

Tavris, C., & Aronson, E. (2015). *Mistakes were made (but not by me)*. Pinter & Martin.

Thalmayer, A. G., Toscanelli, C., & Arnett, J. J. (2021). The neglected 95% revisited: Is American psychology becoming less American? *American Psychologist, 76*, 116–129.

Thomas, K. (1983). *Man and the natural world: A history of the modern sensibility*. Pantheon.

Tierney, J., & Baumeister, R. F. (2019). *The power of bad: How the negativity effect rules us and how we can rule it*. Penguin.

Tiku, N. (2024, December 6). AI friendships claim to cure loneliness. Some are ending in suicide. *Washington Post*. https://www.washingtonpost.com/technology/2024/12/06/ai-companion-chai-research-character-ai/

Tomasello, M. (2019). *Becoming human: A theory of ontogeny*. Belknap Press.

Tooby, J. (2020). Evolutionary psychology as the crystalizing core of a unified modern social science. *Evolutionary Behavioral Sciences, 14*(4), 390–403.

Turnbull, C. (2015). *The forest people*. Random House.

United Nations. (2024, May 6). *UN report: Nature's dangerous decline "unprecedented," species extinction rate accelerating*. https://www.un.org/sustainabledevelopment/blog/2019/05/nature-decline-unprecedented-report/

United Nations Development Programme. (2023). *Human development report*. UNDP.

Uscinski, J. E., & Parent, J. M. (2014). *American conspiracy theories*. Oxford University Press.

Van Bavel, J. J., & Packer, D. J. (2021). *The power of us: Harnessing our shared identities to improve performance, increase cooperation, and promote social harmony*. Little, Brown Spark.

Vandereycken, W., & Deth, R. V. (1994). *From fasting saints to anorexic girls: The history of self-starvation*. Athlone Press.

Van der Meer, T. G., Hameleers, M., & Kroon, A. C. (2020). Crafting our own biased media diets: The effects of confirmation, source, and negativity bias on selective attendance to online news. *Mass Communication and Society*, *23*(6), 937–967.

Volz, L. J., & Gazzaniga, M. S. (2017). Interaction in isolation: 50 years of insights from split-brain research. *Brain*, *140*(7), 2051–2060.

Von Hippel, W., & Trivers, R. (2011). The evolution and psychology of self-deception. *Behavioral and Brain Sciences*, *34*(1), 1.

Vyse, S. A. (2013). *Believing in magic: The psychology of superstition*. Oxford University Press.

Vyse, S. (2022). *The uses of delusion: Why it's not always rational to be rational*. Oxford University Press.

Wallace, C. (2018, August 1). Comfort isn't enough. Be a helper. *Slate*. https://slate.com/human-interest/2018/08/be-a-helper-reassuring-children-about-the-news-isnt-enough.html

Whiting, B. B., Edwards, C. P., Edwards, C. P., & Ember, C. R. (1988). *Children of different worlds: The formation of social behavior*. Harvard University Press.

Williams, H. (1865). *The superstitions of witchcraft*. Longman, Green, Longman, Roberts & Green.

Woolley, J. D., Cornelius, C. A., & Lacy, W. (2011). Developmental changes in the use of supernatural explanations for unusual events. *Journal of Cognition and Culture*, *11*(3–4), 311–337.

Wrangham, R. (2009). *Catching fire: How cooking made us human*. Basic Books.

Yegerov, O. (2019, June 21). These popular Stalin jokes may have been the last word you said. *Russia Beyond*. https://www.rbth.com/history/330551-stalin-jokes-ussr

Zell, E., Strickhouser, J. E., Sedikides, C., & Alicke, M. D. (2020). The better-than-average effect in comparative self-evaluation: A comprehensive review and meta-analysis. *Psychological Bulletin*, *146*, 118–149.

Zuckerman, M. (2007). *Sensation seeking and risk*. American Psychological Association.

Index

For the benefit of digital users, indexed terms that span two pages (e.g., 52–53) may, on occasion, appear on only one of those pages.

Tables and figures are indicated by an italic *t* or *f* following the paragraph number.